# refuge

How "Hospital Church" Ministry
Can Change Your Church Forever

# refuge

How "Hospital Church" Ministry
Can Change Your Church Forever

## James M. Reeves

Kregel
*Academic & Professional*

*Refuge: How "Hospital Church" Ministry Can Change Your Church Forever*

© 2010 James M. Reeves

Published by Kregel Publications, a division of Kregel, Inc., P.O. Box 2607, Grand Rapids, MI 49501.

Unless otherwise indicated, Scripture taken from the NEW AMERICAN STANDARD BIBLE, updated edition. Copyright © 1960, 1962, 1963, 1968, 1971, 1972, 1973, 1975, 1977, 1995 by The Lockman Foundation. Used by permission. (www.Lockman.org)

Scripture quotations marked NIV are from the *Holy Bible, New International Version®*. Copyright © 1973, 1978, 1984 by International Bible Society. Used by permission of Zondervan. All rights reserved.

Scripture quotations marked NKJV are from the New King James Version. Copyright © 1982 by Thomas Nelson, Inc. Used by permission. All rights reserved.

Some names and identifying details have been changed to protect the privacy of individuals.

Library of Congress Cataloging-in-Publication Data
Reeves, James M., 1944-
    Refuge: how "hospital church" ministry can change your church forever /
James M. Reeves; foreword by Stephen Arterburn.
        p. cm.
    1. Pastoral psychology.    2. Celebration Fellowship (Fort Worth, Tex.)
3. Healing—Religious aspects—Christianity.    I. Title.
    BV4012.R44 2010
    253.5—dc22

                                                                2009035533

ISBN 978-0-8254-3573-7

*Printed in the United States of America*
10  11  12  13  14 / 5  4  3  2  1

*I want to dedicate this work to Laura,*
*who is my incredible wife,*
*partner in life and ministry,*
*and hero.*

*And to Tiffany and Zack,*
*the two greatest kids*
*any father could ever dream of having.*

# CONTENTS

# FOREWORD

The recovery movement is dead." How many times have I heard that statement from church leaders, publishers, and even some bookstore retailers? Maybe a few hundred times over the last ten years. Funny, I don't think the rest of the world got the memo. Not so funny: I don't think those inside the church got the memo either.

The truth is, hurt and broken up people are everywhere, outside—and inside—the four walls of the church. Christian leaders have made progress over the last two decades in trying to touch those who are fallen and can't get up.

Many are trying . . . few are succeeding.

Why? Recovery support groups are good; the offer of forgiveness is admirable; counseling is needed . . . but I can honestly say: We still have a church that would rather look the part of Jesus than act the part of Jesus.

We want the appearance of having it together without the substance. We want healthy Christians, but we think the only roadmap is found in the Bible under "spiritual growth." I'm head-over-heels in love with God's Word as a source of healing, but the premise of this book is absolutely true; I've seen it true in a hundred thousand letters and phone calls to *New Life Live*[1]:

---

1. Part of New Life Ministries, *New Life Live!* is a nationally syndicated radio program aired on more than 180 radio stations nationwide.

Spiritual health cannot truly take root if there is not emotional health first.

Dr. James Reeves agrees that what is needed within the church isn't more recovery groups on every addiction imaginable. For twenty years, his church has been what the title of this book says: a refuge. What he's done is create a biblical model of love, concern, honesty, community, help . . . you know, Christianity!

The secret to Dr. Reeves's success in Fort Worth is that he, his leaders, and his congregants admit what many others don't, won't, or can't: that this earth isn't heaven and because of this our land is crawling with messed-up folks who need more genuine love from genuine followers. We don't need a program, we need a heart transplant.

*We need the heart of Jesus.*

New Life Ministries is in contact with churches every day of the year. We hear from addicted pastors, healthy pastors . . . and the addicted and healthy within their walls. Not a church in the United States—perhaps in the world—is immune to the mess a human soul can make. And no simple small group or niche ministry can solve the problem. That's why this book is so important. It's not just giving a challenge to all churches everywhere to get real about emotional health leading to spiritual health; it's giving all leaders everywhere the ideas and tools to make their church a REFUGE church; a place where any messed-up soul (read: everyone) can feel safe, get healing, and then pass it along.

Don't read this book if you want to start another program. Read it if you'd like your church to be a living embodiment of how Christ would create a safe community in your corner of the kingdom.

—Steve Arterburn
Laguna Beach, CA, 2008

# Acknowledgments

Anything accomplished in life that is worth doing is always done in community. This work is no different. There have been so many people who have been a part of this process.

First, I want to thank the incredible people of Celebration Fellowship, the Hospital Church, who for years have been the practitioners of these principles and first encouraged me to write this all down on paper. That body of believers has been the safe place where I and others have been able to experience the healing power of these truths from God's Word.

Then I want to thank Shannon Ethridge. Years ago, Shannon became a friend and encourager to our ministry. It was Shannon who encouraged Greg Johnson to take a look at the manuscript and consider representing me as my literary agent. Without Greg, I doubt that this would ever have become a reality. Thanks, Greg.

I also want to thank Greg for suggesting Marcus Brotherton to help me put this into a form and style that would be acceptable to publishers. Marcus is a consummate professional and has been an encouragement to me in ways that he doesn't even realize.

I also want to thank Steve Arterburn for writing a foreword that is honest, hard-hitting, and to the point. That is my style. I have no doubt that his words had a great deal to do with getting a publisher's attention.

Speaking of publishers, I would be remiss if I didn't mention Kregel Publications for being willing to take a risk on *Refuge* during economic times when publishing, like so many other industries, was so tentative. Thank you, Kregel.

The Willow Creek Association deserves a huge shout out for inviting me to speak about these truths at their Group Life Conference in Chicago. Thank you, Willow, for your impact, not only on this project but also for the gospel all over the world.

So, one after another, person after person, God has used so many to bring this to the point of becoming available to a wider audience. For that I am humbled and grateful.

It is fitting that I end with praise to the Great Physician, Jesus Christ, for His calling to His body, the church, to become a refuge and hospital where He can do His doctoring work. Thank you, Lord Jesus, who is the Alpha and Omega, the Beginning and the End, the First and the Last. Your name is above every name.

INTRODUCTION

INTRODUCTION

# WHY "REFUGE"?

When the twelve tribes of Israel entered into the Promised Land, God divided the land among only eleven of the tribes. The tribe of Levi, the priestly tribe, was the one exception. The Levites were to live scattered throughout the land, spreading their priestly influence among the people.

As part of the plan, Levitical priests were assigned to live in forty-eight cities throughout the land, six of which were designated as "cities of refuge" (Num. 35; Deut. 4:41–43, 19:1–13; Josh. 20). There are so many things about these cities that speak to us about the grace and mercy of God, both then and now. By way of introduction, let me mention three:

First, cities of refuge were places of hope for the hopeless. The common practice of the day was for a person to take matters into his own hands and extract revenge even for the accidental death of a family member or friend. A person being pursued under that practice was without hope. With the establishment of the cities of refuge, there was always hope for the hopeless if only he could enter one of these cities (Num. 35:6, 12).

Second, these cities were places of easy access. The six cities were scattered evenly through the land of Israel so that no one would be more than one day's journey from a place of refuge (Josh. 20:7–8). Roads were to be built to the cities that were twice the normal width of a road, meticulously maintained and clearly marked (Deut. 19:3). There would be no stumbling blocks in the way for the person seeking refuge.

Third, these were places of openness and honesty. Before anyone could be admitted into the city, he had to be willing to confess the manslaughter to the elders of the city (Josh. 20:4).

Scripture says that everything in the Old Testament is fulfilled in Christ (Matt. 5:17). The imagery of the cities of refuge is used in Hebrews 6:17–20, where Jesus Christ is pictured as the One in whom we find refuge and have hope. Since the church is the body of Christ (1 Cor. 12:27), intended to function as His hands and feet and to do what Christ did (Eph. 5:1), then we as the body of Christ must become a refuge. We are in a time of needing to minister to wounded people who are hurting emotionally and spiritually like never before. The church must unqualifiedly become a safe place—a place of help, hope, and healing for all who come.

*Refuge* is a call to the church, the body of Christ, to become the refuge that God intends us to be. It is also, I hope, a map that can help any church chart its course, build its roads, and post signs that unapologetically say, "Welcome to the church. You're in a place of refuge, and you're safe."

PART ONE

# The Background

CHAPTER 1

# A PASSION BIRTHED
# FROM REAL LIFE

The pilgrimage of building a hospital church[1] began
for me on July 24, 1954, the day I was born. In retro-
spect, I can see that God has used everything in my life from that
day forward to prepare me for leading the church I do today,
and for imparting the truths found in this book. It hasn't been
an easy road to get here, but I say with confidence that God has
worked all things together for good (Rom. 8:28). Thankfully, you
don't have to go through what I've been through to help your
church transition to the hospital church model. I hope that the
information that follows helps create a framework to show you
where the principles in this book have come from.

My father was an alcoholic, and my mother was a Jehovah's
Witness. I have often joked that if you looked in the dictionary
under "dysfunctional family," our picture would be there. We

---

1. I use the term "hospital church" to describe a church that people can turn
to for help, hope, and healing. This style of ministry has become so deeply
ingrained in the innovative, Christ-following church I lead—Celebration
Fellowship, in Fort Worth, Texas—that it is just as often called the Hospital
Church.

were off-the-charts dysfunctional. My earliest memories in-
volve a series of moves from one small town to the next.
Sometimes we stayed only a few days. I was always the new kid
in school. One of our longer stays was six months in a motel on
the outskirts of Cortez, Colorado, when I was in second grade.
That move was also one of the happier ones for me because I
made a friend or two. Friends were rare for me in those early
years.

When my father worked, he was an oilfield roughneck on
drilling rigs. His pattern was to work just long enough to make
enough money to go on a drinking binge. Whenever he stopped
showing up for work, he lost his job, and we packed up and
moved to the next town. I honestly cannot remember ever
seeing my dad sober.

Dad was often gone for days. Whenever he showed up, my
mother questioned him about where he had been. Things got
heated and turned violent. My sister and I often tried to defend
our mom. I guess seeing us stand next to her with our tiny fists
doubled up looked pretty funny, because it usually made Dad
laugh. Then the beatings stopped.

At age seven, I remember walking with Mom around town
looking for Dad's beat-up car. When we found it parked outside
of some local dive, she sent me in to fish him out. This happened
several times. Sometimes Dad came. Sometimes he didn't.

When I was eight, Mom had finally had enough and left him.
The three of us ended up in a small West Texas town in a one-
bedroom, tin-roofed shack on a dirt road, across from the town
cemetery. My mother had dropped out of high school after her
sophomore year to marry Dad, so she had no formal education
or work skills. She ended up waiting tables in a truck stop restaurant for fifty cents an hour, plus tips. I had never been supervised
much up to this point, but from then on I was definitely on my
own. I went to school when I wanted to. I found something else to
do with amazing regularity. Often I spent my days just wandering
the streets. Sometimes I explored abandoned houses. Somehow
I managed to show up enough to get passed through the system
without ever failing a grade. That's a wonder, considering I went

to three different schools in three different towns during first grade alone.

When I was ten, my mother married a good man with a decent job whom she had met at the restaurant. We moved out of our shack to a better part of town. My stepfather tried to provide a sense of order and discipline to my life, but by that time I was beyond control. The stress of taking on a wife and two kids, one of whose behavior was off the charts, proved too much for him. He had a nervous breakdown and landed in a hospital within a year of taking us on.

Experimenting with drugs and alcohol came very early for me. I honestly can't even remember when it began—certainly before I was a teenager. I had been born into an environment of chemical abuse, and it seemed natural for me to follow. It was the 1960s then, and anyone could score drugs at will. I started going to school stoned. Soon I was skipping school and getting stoned. Then I was out at night getting stoned. Sometimes I stayed out for days. I was in and out of trouble with local law enforcement. It was an insane way of living, but everything seemed normal to me.

## WHEN EVERYTHING CHANGED

By the end of my junior year of high school, I found myself pretty much alone. I had been running with a crowd of kids who were all one to two years older than me. But one by one they had all been busted for drug possession or had quit school and then been drafted and sent to Vietnam. Into that relationship void God sent some Christian young people who reached out to me. I played guitar and sang, and they were all musical. They simply began to include me. They did life in a way I had never been exposed to. I was fascinated and drawn to it. They never preached to me, but they were never bashful about expressing their love for Christ. Mostly, they just cared about me, in spite of how messed up I was. Their families took me in. Their homes were open to me day and night. I went from not knowing what a family looked like to being surrounded by several great ones.

My spiritual life came to a head on New Year's Eve, 1971, in a lodge in Cloudcroft, New Mexico. It was during a youth retreat. I had been going to church with my new friends for several months, much to the chagrin of my Jehovah's Witness mother, who couldn't decide if the trade-off was worth it. On the one hand, the police weren't bringing me home at three in the morning anymore, I wasn't throwing up in my sleep from alcohol poisoning, and I wasn't tripping on acid or smoking dope. On the other hand, I was keeping tight company with these "religious people" who from her perspective (since they weren't JWs) were all part of the great whore of Babylon.

I had heard the gospel several times before, yet that night at the retreat I glimpsed firsthand how the Good News could be for me. Right there in a very simple way I said to God, "If you can do anything with this mess of my life, I give it to you right now." There were no bells or whistles, but I knew I was made new in Christ. When I stood and told people I had accepted Christ, the house came down. Everybody had been praying for me for months. There was hugging and crying and all kinds of celebrating. It was a great welcome to my new family in Christ.

I had never known any purpose other than to party and get high, but almost immediately I began to sense a desire to do ministry. I didn't have the slightest clue what that meant, except that I wanted to reach other kids just like me.

Four months after I accepted Christ, I graduated from high school—just barely. My final semester was the first time I had ever cared about school or made an attempt to learn.

One of my new friends was headed off to a small Christian college that seemed to accept anybody as long as you had a high school diploma and could pay the tuition. I secured a job and some grants and loans. The morning I left for college I went to my mom's room at 5:30 AM and woke her. "Mom, I'm going to college," I said.

"Oh, is that today?" she answered. "Well, be good."

That was my send-off.

When I got to campus, I was shocked to see all the parents with U-Haul trailers moving their kids into the dormitory.

There was all kinds of crying and sobbing. I remember feeling a deep sense of loneliness. No one there was crying over me. But I stuffed the feelings deep inside me and carried on. There was no sense dwelling on anything emotional, I figured. That was all in the past, I thought. I was set to win the world for Christ.

One month later, my father died. I hadn't seen him for several months. The last time I had seen him alive he had taken me to a local dive to drink and shoot pool, but I had just become a Christian and said I didn't want to go in. Instead, we sat outside in his old junker and talked. He sipped out of a tall boy in a brown paper bag and asked me why I was going to church all of a sudden. We got into an argument because he said it was only to meet girls, and he dropped me off at home. That was our last meeting.

Dad had been found on the floor of his room in a local flophouse. He had no identification on him. He hadn't eaten in days. He was penniless—he'd spent every cent he had on booze. He died of kidney failure caused by acute alcoholism. He was forty-one.

The burial was the next day. My family looked to me for what to do. Dad had been raised a Jehovah's Witness by my grandmother, but he had been disfellowshipped for years, and no one would have anything to do with him. If anything was going to be done, it would fall to me, the only son. So, on a Saturday afternoon when I was eighteen, I performed my first funeral—for my father.

I don't remember much I said that day. The graveside service was only about ten minutes long. The only people there were my new Christian friends, my sister, and my grandmother. I do remember saying that my father was a picture of what the world would do to you if you gave yourself to it. I called his situation as truthfully as I saw it—his was a wasted life. I was so thankful that Christ had found me and saved me from becoming like my dad. That was all. Then they buried him.

The morning after the funeral, I pressed on. I joined a weekend revival team from my college. We were assigned to a small West Texas church. There were three team members:

a student preacher, a worship leader, and me. My job was to play guitar, sing, and give my testimony. I had a lot to tell that Sunday. Monday morning I was back in class. I didn't need any time off, I concluded—my dad's death didn't affect me. At least that was what I whispered to myself. After all, I had been saved and changed by Christ, and I had a world to win.

After two years at college, I had raised my grades enough to transfer to Baylor University. I attended Baylor for six weeks before I realized my mother didn't know I was there. I had been on my own since I was a boy. It didn't seem strange to me to not tell her I had moved.

At Baylor, I majored in Greek and began to hit my stride. I realized for the first time that I had some academic ability. I even made the dean's list. I graduated and served in ministry capacities at a couple of churches for the next two years. I wasn't sure where I would end up. I went to law school at night for a while, wondering if it was for me. I loved law school, but I knew that practicing law was not my calling.

I started seminary in Fort Worth in 1978. The next summer, I married my wife Laura, who, for the last thirty years of marriage has been my hero and best friend. I still cannot believe that God would bless me with someone like her. Her strength, character, integrity, compassion, and talent never cease to amaze and inspire me. Her unconditional love and acceptance has been a huge component in my emotional healing process.

## HOW IT ALL BLEW UP

When I graduated from seminary in 1981, Laura and I went to my first pastorate, a dying church comprised of a handful of elderly folks. They loved the Lord, and they loved me and my young wife. The first year, we saw more than one hundred people come to Christ. I was paraded across the stage during the annual Florida Baptist convention as the pastor of one of the top ten fastest growing churches in the state based on baptism-to-membership ratio. Everyone applauded me as one of the up and coming young stars on the Baptist horizon. (That kind of thing repulses me today, but I have to admit it was pretty exciting at the time.) I was on the fast track never looking back. They had no idea of the emotional train wreck that was in my future.

Neither did I.

After three years at the church in Florida, we moved, and I became the first pastor of a new church plant on the east side of Fort Worth, Texas. We settled into a routine over the next seven years of doing ministry as we had been taught how to do it. The results were nominal. People came in the front door and walked out the back. Each time I would try to do something innovative or different I would face opposition from leadership. Those were years of frustration, fighting, and questioning if I wanted to continue for the long haul in pastoral ministry.

As I moved into my mid-thirties, I began to have more doubts. I spiraled into a depression. A dark cloud descended on me that I felt powerless to lift. All of the emotional issues that related to my dad, my childhood, and my lifestyle before I met Christ began to pop up. These issues had been stuffed beneath the surface for years. I felt anger, guilt, regret, sadness—these feelings combined with the frustration of being stuck in a ministry style I knew didn't fit. It all swirled together to form a raging river of destruction in my life.

The ironic thing was that this was a period when I was being more faithful to the Christian disciplines than I had ever been. I didn't know what else to do. That was the answer I had been giving to others for years when they struggled in their lives: Just do more—pray more, give more, study more, serve more! Just more, and more, and more. I was praying more, studying more, and memorizing more Scripture than ever. I memorized entire books of the Bible! I could quote James, Philippians, and Ephesians word for word. I prayed for hours and hours for God to deliver me from my pain and depression.

But it just kept getting worse.

At the time I couldn't understand why I wasn't getting better—particularly with all I was doing. I now understand that my problem at its core wasn't first a spiritual problem but an emotional problem. That insight forms the core of what this book and the hospital church ministry are all about. But at the time I just didn't get it.

I am five-foot-eleven and weigh about 150 pounds. During this period I dropped to 130. I couldn't sleep at night but strangely longed to crawl in bed and sleep all the time. Yet I continued to muddle through my responsibilities by sheer force of will. I was preaching weekly, doing pastoral ministry, trying to lead the church, working on my Doctor of Ministry degree, and counseling depressed people—all the time getting more and more depressed myself.

One Sunday morning in 1991, things got so bad that when I stood up before the people to preach I felt so overwhelmed I knew I couldn't continue. "I can't do this today," I announced, and left. I had my notes and was prepared to preach, but I knew I didn't have the physical or emotional strength to go on. When I walked out, I got in my car, drove home, and went to bed. As I pulled the covers over my head, I thought, "Well now you've really stepped in it. You're not only depressed, but now you're going to be unemployed." Strangely enough, that thought brought a huge sense of relief.

This is where it gets really crazy: The next morning, I went to the office and started my week, same as usual. Nobody said anything about what had happened! It was simply never talked about. Some people who were freaked out by what I had done didn't come back the next week, but mostly I was the elephant in the room. People must have thought that if they didn't acknowledge my problems, the problems would go away on their own, or maybe I would go away. I desperately needed help, but we weren't the kind of church where anyone could get that kind of help—especially not the senior pastor. I was supposed to have it all together. So I pressed on.

The church met in a school at the time, while we were constructing our first building. I decided I would keep working long enough to get the church into that new building and then resign. I was finished. Two weeks after we moved into the new building I offered my resignation letter to the elders. It was

February 1992. I thought they would shout hallelujah and throw a party. Instead, they suggested that I take some time off and reconsider my decision. They graciously offered me a ninety-day paid sabbatical leave. I didn't think that the church could survive without a pastor for that long after so recently moving into a new building, so I took a two-week vacation instead. I hadn't had a vacation in years.

I decided I would spend the first week of my vacation in a nearby seminary library, praying, reading, and pleading with God. If He wanted me to continue, He needed to show me how. The second week I would take my family away somewhere, then the plan was to come back and reissue my resignation. I didn't have much hope.

Truly, I was at the end of myself. I have since told hundreds of people that being at the end is a great place to be. It's only when we get to the end of ourselves that we can really come to the beginning of God. I was there. I think the Lord knew that if He didn't give me something to hold onto immediately, I wouldn't make it through the week.

On Monday, 8:00 AM, I hit the books in the seminary library. I began by rereading what the New Testament says about the church. Who are we? What are we supposed to look, smell, and taste like? You know, what has Jesus called the church to be?

What happened over those first couple of hours was nothing short of miraculous. I began to sense a spark deep inside me that quickly became a strange sort of flame. I was reading about the church through new eyes—not the eyes of my denomination, or the professional training I had received about how to do church, but through the eyes of desperation.

## THE START OF A NEW LIFE

Those eyes of desperation let me begin to see again what God had called me to and prepared me for. The vision and passion for the church to become a hospital (although I didn't use that term yet) began to take shape in me that morning. I spent the rest of the week in the library rereading Scripture and devouring books on church growth, community, and every subject

I could find that had anything to do with the church. I saw everything through a new filter.

It was a strange place to be: at the end of that week, my passion was renewed, but I still knew I couldn't keep going as I was. I spent the next week with my family, then came back and reissued my resignation. I explained to the leaders what had happened during the week in the library and described the kind of church I wanted to lead and be a part of. My intention was to go out and start another church. Their response shocked me: "Let's do it here." We spent hours discussing what that would mean. In the end I agreed, on the condition that each elder would make the trip through the transition with me. I knew we were in for some difficult days ahead. People never respond well to change. The elders agreed.

I spent four Sunday evenings walking the congregation through the principles the changes were built upon. The church embraced the idea of transitioning to this model. It was hard for anyone to find anything to argue with because everything we were about to do had a firm basis in Scripture.

When we began to make some of the changes, however, the struggle began. Some very good people soon left the church. I had one family, who I had been very close to, tell me I had gone absolutely crazy. I considered that an ironic statement. I knew exactly what crazy looked like: It was me trying to be a pastor under the old model. But with the new hospital church model I was more sane than I had ever been in my life.

Over the next few seasons things looked pretty bleak. The numbers kept going down. We hadn't started with a very big crowd in the first place. I wasn't sure if we were going to make it. Change is always hard.

But around Easter we hit the turning point. People were getting it. I was getting it. God began to send people who connected with the vision—real change began to happen. And the rest, as they say, is history.

We've had our ups and downs over the years as any church does—times of growth, times of hitting the wall. But since that inception of the hospital church model we've grown in our understanding of what it means to be a safe church. We have seen emotionally fractured people move toward wholeness. We have seen marriages saved, addicts walk in sobriety, and people who were hopeless find hope. We've seen people like me experience healing from their past. I look back on what we understood when we began this process and compare it with what we understand today, and I realize we didn't have much of a clue back then. But God honored our steps in the right direction. He taught us and protected us as we navigated the treacherous waters of change.

For me personally, these past seventeen years of ministering in the hospital church model have been times of great personal growth and healing. In some areas, I've experienced tremendous personal growth and healing. In other areas, it's come more gradually. I wouldn't be honest if I didn't acknowledge both. Complete emotional healing hasn't come overnight to me—or to anyone in the church. It's a process that comes over time. But through it all it has been wonderful to be a part of a church where I could walk through that personal process openly, without fear, and with the love and support of the body of Christ.

I see now that what I was doing for many years was just putting a spiritual Band-Aid on a severed emotional artery. As I've been transparent with others, I have found new emotional healing and maturity, and my capacity for a deeper intimacy with people and God has grown more than I could have ever dreamed. I have also been blessed to watch hundreds of others walk that path over the past years. The truths of what we've learned form the core of this book and our ministry.

It is my prayer and my desire that as you read the following pages, something will ignite within you as it did in me that Monday in the library. Maybe God will plant this vision in your heart to be a part of a hospital church or to lead one. If what we have learned along the way can benefit you, we've accomplished this stage of our mission. Our gratefulness rests with the Great Physician, Jesus Christ.

CHAPTER 2

# The Hospital Church

After you've been in ministry for a while—the place where you want people to walk closer to Christ—you find out that the world can be a messy, messy place.

You already know that. You wouldn't be reading this book if you didn't. You're a leader, a Christ follower, someone passionate about making a difference in your community and spiritual assembly. You care desperately about reaching people with the good news of Jesus Christ. And if the veil between what's seen and not seen could be pulled back, your hands and feet would show the blood and grime from working with people who desperately need help.

But here's the problem: what you're doing has had a limited effect. You've seen it. You know it. You're probably discouraged. And you wonder what to do.

The problem takes shape like this: Too many times Christian leaders, even without realizing it, offer Band-Aid solutions to full-blown, hemorrhaging wounds. Needy people come to us with bleeding, gushing injuries, and we offer simplistic or misdirected answers, answers that fail to address the root of their issues.

Answers like:

- Just keep coming to church.
- Just join a small group.
- Just learn better communications skills.
- Just come to the retreat.
- Just go for counseling.
- Just read the Bible and pray more.
- Just try harder to be a cleaner, nicer, more mature person.

These are the tools we use, because they are the only tools we know how to use. We find that people often ignore our advice. But even if they follow it for a while, nothing seems to change permanently in their lives. The same harmful, hurtful patterns are repeated again and again.

Have you experienced this in ministry? I have. I experienced it within myself. And I know it's easy to grow disheartened when this happens. When the line of people needing support doesn't get any shorter, it's easy to become weary of trying to help. Sometimes the same people who were at the front of the line circle around and join the end again. After a time of seeing the pattern of programs and advice not working, we begin to feel that our only hope is found in running away. We think: If we could just step off the ministry treadmill for a while—a month, a season, maybe a few years. Maybe we should stop being, say, a small group leader? Or maybe we should switch churches and go somewhere that we can be anonymous? If we're pastors, we toy with switching careers entirely. Maybe we should go install drywall for a while. That would be easier—wouldn't it?

There is hope. Another solution emerges when we stop viewing the church through faulty paradigms. Sometimes these faulty paradigms are unspoken—the false truths people operate under. "If you just love Jesus enough, your pain is going to go away," for instance. Or, "If you are struggling in some area of your life you, just need to have more faith." Or, "If you still struggle with resentment over something that has happened in your life, you must not be very spiritual." Whatever the faulty paradigms are, articulated or not, they need to change.

Perhaps the most crucial paradigm shift boils down to this: Lasting change begins in people's lives when we stop viewing the church as a community of respectability—and start viewing the church as a hospital for the hurting. We are all hurt at some level.

Do you know what I mean by a community of respectability? It is a church where nicely dressed people come and speak nicely to each other, and sing nice songs, and hear nice messages, and volunteer to lead nice programs for nice children, and go home and have nice jobs, and engage in nice hobbies and act nicely to their families throughout the week. Does any of that describe your church?

Lasting change begins when we start viewing the church as a hospital—a place that frequently sees the guts and gore of real life; that is filled with people slowly dying from the cancer of emotional pain, the burns of broken relationships, and amputations of unfulfilled dreams; that keeps a ready supply of emotional IVs and spiritual heart monitors on hand; and where all people, ultimately, can find hope and healing through Jesus Christ. Does that describe your church?

If it doesn't, it needs to—or will need to soon. Not only because the hospital church model is a proven way of reaching lost and hurting people. But because it's the next huge paradigm for effective church ministry. Let me forecast the future. This vision may sound strong or arrogant, but I say it out of humble concern over the reality of the woundedness I'm seeing all around me today. If the principles (not a program) outlined in this book are not adopted in a church, I predict that that church will stumble badly within the next fifteen to twenty years.

Think of it this way. Remember how twenty to thirty years ago the big paradigm shift was to contemporary church music? A church either had to switch from singing hymns to a contemporary style of worship or it got left behind.

A similar paradigm shift is upon us today, but it goes much further than people's music preferences. We live in a new, Internet-fueled world where addiction, pain, and destruction have been made easier to slide into than ever. The people we need to reach have a skewed understanding of morality, maturity, ethics, and truth like we've never seen before. If we are ever going to reach this generation, then we must reach them in all their chaos. We must offer people a safe place to experience emotional healing along with spiritual healing. The church today must become a hospital.

That's the message of this book.

It's change, or die.

## A HOSPITAL—AT OUR CHURCH?

As I teach various seminars around the country about the concepts of what it means to develop a hospital church, I frequently encounter this common response: *What? Our church doesn't have any real problems—certainly not like the ones you're describing. Isn't the whole idea that a church needs to be a hospital a little extreme?*

I understand the initial resistance to the idea. If your church isn't used to seeing hurting people, then it's hard to believe the people in your midst are wounded. My daughter, Tiffany, works as a pediatric nurse in a large-scale city hospital, the only pediatric hospital in a five-state area that's received a level one trauma designation (with a trauma surgical team ready twenty-four hours a day). Every day she sees young patients flown in by helicopter and rushed in by ambulance. Some suffer from sicknesses that threaten their lives. Others are victims of accidents or abuse. She recently treated a child whose mother threw him and his brother off a bridge in Dallas. All patients who come to this hospital have two things in common: they are hurting, and they need immediate care. There's no question in Tiffany's mind about who the hurting people are.

Few churches have erected something like a sign that says "level one trauma facility" over the front door—either literally or in their vision statement. The push to create communities of respectability is subtle yet powerful, and much more widespread than we think. Because of this, the wounded stay hidden in the pew (or chairs if you are more contemporary).

The Bible states that all humans are involved in a great battle. It rages all around us. Our enemy doesn't drop bombs or shoot semiautomatic weapons in this war. Yet he is more dedicated, vicious, and deadly than any human enemy could ever be. Ours is a spiritual war. It sometimes leaves physical scars but more often leaves emotional scars—scars that are harder to see but that touch the very deepest parts of the human soul. Throughout the New Testament we are reminded and warned, not only about the reality of our enemy but also the seriousness of this battle we are fighting. Consider these verses:

> Our struggle is not against flesh and blood, but against the rulers, against the powers, against the world forces of this darkness, against the spiritual forces of wickedness in the heavenly places. (Eph. 6:12)

> Be on the alert. Your adversary, the devil, prowls around like a roaring lion, seeking someone to devour. (1 Peter 5:8)

> The thief comes . . . to steal and kill and destroy. (John 10:10)

Chances are good that you are no stranger to this war. Its effects are evident everywhere you look. Many people are simply unwilling to acknowledge them. Perhaps you've seen it in your family. Or you've seen it in yourself. This war has been raging since the beginning of time, and it's getting more intense as we walk toward the end times. God created the first man and woman in perfection. In the Garden of Eden, Adam and Eve enjoyed a perfect environment and perfect fellowship with a perfect Creator (Gen. 2:29–31). And Satan succeeded in destroying that perfection. Eden was locked up, and Adam and Eve were kicked out (Gen. 3:24). They lost their perfect fellowship with the Creator. The same enemy who fights against us is the one who did that to them, and he wants to continue doing it today.

The good news is that Satan is not ultimately victorious in this war. The Bible shows how God has worked through history to provide a way back into perfect fellowship with Him. That work was accomplished in the death, burial, and resurrection of Jesus Christ,

God's Son. It is through Christ, and Christ alone, that we gain the potential of abundant life here and now (John 10:10), and the promise of eternal life when our time on earth ends (John 3:16).

Satan's plan is now to stop a person from coming to eternal life, or, if that fails, to sabotage a person's abundant life. That's the war that wages today. In it, Satan uses a variety of strategies. The wounds from this war sometimes come from sinful choices that we make. Sometimes wounds are inflicted on us by others who make sinful choices. Some wounds come from the fact that we live in a fallen world where bad and hurtful things happen. It's safe to say that all people are wounded to one degree or another. No one escapes the effects of this war.

The realization that we are all in this war together is vital in beginning to see the need for every church to become a hospital church. Some wounds are overt—they are obvious immediately when people are airlifted to our churches from accident sites. But other wounds are much harder to see. They are layered over with years of Band-Aid solutions, yet they're just as life-threatening as the obvious ones, and they hurt just as much.

A true hospital church begins when we start to view ourselves not as white-coated professionals with clipboards and all the answers but as patients lying in wards next to other wounded people. Perhaps we are a bit further along in our healing and know how to help the patient next to us push his call button to get a nurse's attention, but it's important to recognize and accept that we are all patients in the hospital together. We are all wounded healers, all having fallen short of the glory of God, all saved by grace (Rom. 3:23–24). The Physician is Jesus Christ. He is the one Doctor. Our task is not to be the doctor instead of Him, or to try to heal people ourselves, but rather to be a safe people who provide a safe place with a safe process for patients to experience His healing hand.

## THE ISSUE WITHIN

The hospital church ministry I'm presenting in this book is not a model for recovery ministry, not in the traditional sense anyway. The term *recovery ministry* conjures up images of substance addictions, and people tend to make snap judgments about what recovery ministry looks like based on those images.

I call the hospital church style ministry a model of support ministry. Support ministry encompasses a traditional recovery ministry model, but it extends further. A person doesn't have to be addicted to drugs or alcohol to benefit from a support ministry model. Support ministry extends to every person in a church. We've all been emotionally wounded somewhere along the line. We must all deal with the issues that have created mistrust, bitterness, fear, resentment—all the things that affect our capacity to have soul-to-soul, heart-to-heart, intimate relationships in our lives. As we experience emotional healing, the ceiling is raised on our capacity to enter into a deeper, more intimate relationship with the Father—what every person longs for.

In a nutshell, the hospital church model means that a church becomes a safe place for people to come and heal. Safety is the vital component. And it's the one component that is sorely lacking in most churches today.

Of all the communities in existence, the church is supposed to be the safest place for hurting people to receive love. Sadly, for too many, the church is the last place where people feel they can be vulnerable. There's the fear of being judged for imperfections. There's also the confidentiality factor—fear that word of weaknesses will spread through the congregation like wildfire. Instead of being allowed to share the truth about themselves, shame keeps people from receiving the healing they so desperately need.

Here are a few stories of people who have approached our church lately. If these people came to your church, how might your church help?

John and his wife, Patty, came to us five years ago. They had been actively involved in a good Bible-believing church until their teenage son, Chris, started using meth. John and Patty went to their pastor, who didn't know how to help. The pastor didn't have any recovering alcoholics in his church (that he knew of) who could partner with their son for accountability and support. The pastor had never been trained how to hold an intervention. There was no system in his church designed to address the pain John and Patty were experiencing, and certainly no system set up to help the drug-addicted son.

Jeff and Christy are in their late twenties and want to begin a family. Both are Christians now, but before she was saved, Christy led a fairly wild life and contracted an STD that left her unable to have children. The couple doesn't know who to talk to or what to do. They don't feel they can share this information in their small group. It's filled with young, affluent parents who look like they have it all together. Jeff and Christy don't want to be branded as the odd couple.

Sean is in his early thirties, married, with two young daughters. He's recently started a new business and is under a lot of pressure. He loves his wife, but she's never been, in his words, "very supportive of him." Sean has found that the "only" outlet for him is Internet pornography. It started out with some casual looking, but now it's an every-night occurrence. He feels out of control. He's lost his self-respect. His wife isn't talking to him. His business is about to go under. His pastor suggested going on a men's retreat. Sean went—and the experience was good—but it was just one weekend out of a year. He needs a lot more ongoing support than his church is capable of providing.

Beverley is a Christian woman in her mid-fifties. She's never worked outside of her home, and now that her kids are both grown, she wonders what to do with a lot of her day. Her doctor has diagnosed depression. Her pastor suggested counseling. Beverley has been to counseling and is on antidepressants, but she longs for just one good friend she can really talk to. She attends the women's Bible Study at her church every Tuesday morning, but somehow that never seems like enough.

Susan, thirty-four, is what leaders sometimes refer to as "an extra grace required" person. She has three children, all fathered by different boyfriends, and receives state assistance to pay her rent and utility bills. Susan grew up as a foster child and never received much instruction on how to become an adult. Mostly, she approached the church looking for help with her kids, ages seventeen, nine, and two. The oldest attended youth group once or twice, but it wasn't for him, Susan said. The middle one likes Sunday school, but teachers complain she's out of control. The youngest, a boy, goes to the nursery, but workers are concerned because he often hits other kids and comes with a runny nose and cough.

I could tell so many stories like this, stories of wounded people caught in a wash of chaos. These people want help but don't know where to turn. Often they hop around from church to church. For a season, the new church feels good. A honeymoon stage takes place when a person feels something exciting, new, and hope-filled. But a person's problems are never truly addressed by changing an outward environment.

When people go from church to church, they are looking outside themselves for a solution. But the problem is inside. Real change will never happen unless people confront the woundedness in their lives. True spiritual growth can't happen unless the church becomes a safe place for people to admit their struggles and pain.

What's needed is a hospital church.

**TO THE ROOT**

Dream with me for a moment. Imagine your church is a place of healing, safety, and acceptance. It's a place where marriages are repaired, families are reconciled, addicts are freed from dependency upon harmful substances and behaviors, and people are transformed to be all God called them to be.

This is God's call to every church.

Sometimes people oppose this idea, believing that churches are only called to spread the gospel of Jesus Christ. They argue that a church's main job is to get people into heaven—period. Once people are saved, the rest of life takes care of itself, right?

My answer is that the church has a dual role—and both roles are intricately linked. God's call to the church is *spiritual*, yes. We are called to show people the pathway to eternal life through faith in Jesus Christ. God's call to the church is also *emotional*. Although faith in Christ provides immediate forgiveness for sin and the promise of eternal life, sin causes emotional wounds in each and every one of us. If emotional healing does not take place, these wounds can block us from fully experiencing the abundant life God offers to those who believe in Him (more on this in chapter 4). Facilitating emotional healing is a vital role of a church, for in so doing it opens the pathway to spiritual abundance.

These two callings are not in conflict. In fact, a church can't have one without the other. Together, they lead to the goal of greater intimacy with others and the Lord. But we cannot address one issue and ignore the other. Jesus, the Great Physician, calls His church to become a hospital where He can do His total healing work. A hospital church is a place where people receive both spiritual healing from the eternal effects of sin and emotional healing from the temporal effects of sin.

I want church leaders everywhere to have the knowledge, vision, and tools to transform their churches into safe places. Safe places are where people can tell their secrets and be honest. They say things like, "This is what I'm experiencing on the inside—and I've never told anybody this until now."

When people start telling their secrets in a safe environment and applying biblical principles of healing to the wounds of the past, real change begins to happen. When someone doesn't deal with the wounds of the past, then they aren't the past. They are the present and will color the future. Most of our wounds have an emotional source but also have both emotional and spiritual consequences.

Often the biggest step that each of us needs to take is to forgive. We will never be free from the pain of our past until we release the people who hurt us. Forgiveness frees us from bitterness and resentment. It is the vital step to emotional healing. (I'll say more about this in chapter 9.)

When people forgive others, they experience emotional healing at their core because they are released from things such as bitterness and resentment. And when this happens, people can begin to experience true intimacy with others. They relearn how to trust other people. And in relearning how to trust others, they discover how to trust God, the source of real transformation.

Those are the kinds of issues we want to talk about in this book: How emotional wounds affect our relationship with others as well as our relationship to the heavenly Father. How the church can become a safe place for people to experience healing so they can enjoy all the benefits of both their horizontal relationships and their vertical relationship to the Father.

The questions are: What does a safe church look like? And how can your church begin to operate this way?

## A CHURCH THAT WORKS

For the past seventeen years, I have had the privilege of leading a hospital church called Celebration Fellowship in Fort Worth, Texas. We transitioned into this support ministry model in 1992. Since that time, I have come to realize that there is no other type of ministry that I would ever want to be a part of again.

The backbone of our hospital church has been developing what are called freedom groups within the church. A freedom group is a place where people can be honest and open without fear of reprisal or condemnation. It's where they can tell their secret sins, fears, resentments, and life experiences—many of which they've previously hidden. Think of a freedom group as a transparency group. It's where people are seen and known. That's when healing starts to happen—when people stop keeping secrets.

A freedom group is different from what's traditionally called a small group. Small groups are usually where life and ministry take place. In a small group, people study the Bible;

talk; pray; eat; reach out to their neighborhoods; and discuss issues related to their lives such as parenting, communication, and relationships. If people have needs such as meals after the birth of a child or a visit before surgery, they call the members of their small group. A freedom group meets different needs. It's a group set up for a specific length of time (usually twelve to fourteen weeks) intentionally designed to facilitate emotional healing.

We have both small groups (we call them community groups) and freedom groups in our church. Whenever any new person comes through our front door, we attempt to steer him or her to a freedom group first. It's not a law that a person must go into a freedom group first, but we emphasize recovery and healing for everyone. A freedom group is billed as the place to start.

Too often I've seen people walk into a small group without dealing with some of their emotional woundedness first. When that happens, it can hurt what's happening in the small group.

It's disastrous to take people who are emotionally stunted in their capacity for intimate relationships of trust and caring and put them into small groups that are designed for that purpose. They recoil and withdraw, sometimes striking out verbally or emotionally at those around them. They can suck the life out of a small group and end up discouraged themselves. They know they don't fit in and are frustrated by it. Others know they don't fit in and are frustrated by it.

If a church offers small groups only, it stops one level too short. People need community, but the tools of true community need to develop in a special kind of group first. Freedom groups allow emotional healing to begin so people can function within the communities that small groups facilitate.

I want to encourage everybody reading this book that freedom groups are not simply add-ons to the other programs in your church. Rather, freedom groups need to form the core of your church. This may be the most radical thing I hold to: Freedom groups need to be the entry point and underpinning of every other ministry of your church.

Why? When churches create separate programs for emotionally wounded people, those programs tend to be seen as the place for the "sickos." If your church has recovery groups, it's easy to think, "Well, those groups are for other people, but certainly not me." It sets up a hierarchy or caste system: the sick and the well, the good and the bad. In essence, the goal is not just to create safe *places* but to create a safe *church*.

Freedom groups really work, and the church becomes a haven when we understand we're all emotionally wounded in one way or another. The fall affected us all. Yes, we have been hurt at different levels, but we're all sinners saved by grace—and we've all been affected by the sins of others. We're all in process. Freedom groups are for everyone from the senior leaders down. That is, unless there is someone in our midst who has no issues, needs no healing, and struggles with nothing in this life. But then, Jesus had words for people who claimed that, didn't He? *Hypocrites, white-washed tombs.* Ouch!

I want to offer a specific encouragement to pastors and church board members reading this book: Much of the success or failure of developing the hospital church model in your church will depend on the amount of support you give it. A hospital church model will flourish only when it has the complete support of the decision makers. And not just support but involvement in the process. You will benefit personally, and you will be saying very clearly, "This is a safe place, even for leaders."

If you're reading this book and you're not a pastor or a church board member, what should you do? Well, I'm a senior pastor, and I know what it feels like when people throw books at me, inform me I need to read them, and then walk out of the church if I don't. Leaders don't respond well to that approach. As a layperson you carry influence in your local assembly whether you realize it or not, and God calls you to tactfully and gently help set the vision in your church. Specifically how you do that will require much prayer and thoughtfulness. Let me suggest two places to start. If your pastors or board members are open to reading this book, then good, start there. If you don't sense they are open to that, then ask if you can summarize the findings of this book and present your findings to them at a meeting or over lunch. Good things often take place when you talk things out first. Approach them humbly, with respect and appreciation for who they are and what they do. Then volunteer yourself to be available in any way you are needed.

In the pages ahead I want to communicate the need, the biblical basis, and some how-tos for developing a hospital church ministry in your church. This book casts an overall vision for developing a freedom group ministry. It lays the foundations for why the groups are necessary and gives you parameters for setting up the groups in your church.

However, I want to be clear about two things this book *doesn't* do. First, it doesn't show you every specific for implementing this model in your local assembly. Why? Because there's always a danger in providing one tightly woven, inflexible plan that's supposed to fit every church in North America. Undoubtedly your church has unique distinctives that reflect differences in region, demographics, socioeconomic levels, traditions, histories, and personality types represented in your congregation. The plans laid out in this book can be adapted to fit your particular assembly.

Second, this book does not walk you through the specifics of what to do within the freedom groups. Why? Because there are many other good resources that do that already. Some resources are featured in the appendix at the back of this book. My encouragement is for you to find curriculum to meet the specific needs of your assembly, and of each freedom group.

## HOPE AHEAD

I recently went to a conference where I ended up sharing the hospital church vision with several hundred people. I didn't plan to. I wasn't the main speaker at that conference. I just started talking with whomever I was with at lunch and breaks about what's happening at Celebration Fellowship. Word spread, and pretty soon the hospital church was the talk of the conference.

People came up to me, complete strangers, and asked: "Do those things really happen at your church? Do people really talk about those things?" I saw hope in their eyes, an anticipation that things could be different.

Let me offer you some of that same hope: your church can be more than it is now. Your church can become a place of healing and safety. And when that happens, the people you minister to will truthfully begin to deal with the issues they know are hindering them. There's going to be a new joy. A new level of worship and Bible study. A new level of outreach and effectiveness in ministering to your community. People are going to be set free from what's hindering them and grow closer to God.

A hospital church helps people to experience healing from the wounds of their pasts. When that healing begins, people are set free to mature in Christ, to develop intimacy with the Father, and to live the lives God intended. That's the goal of the hospital church: intimacy with God through healing and freedom. It doesn't matter if we wear the title of pastor or not. That's the business we're all in as ministers of Jesus Christ.

And I can think of no better business to be in than that.

# PART TWO

# The Benefits

CHAPTER 3

# RAW AND NAKED JOY

This chapter was born out of my observation of what I call the "calf eyeing a new gate" response. The calf sees the juicy green grass on the other side of the gate, but the calf is fairly sure that traveling beyond the gate is a bad, bad idea. It's new. It's scary.

I often see this same look in the eyes of people I teach about these hospital church ministry principles. People are interested and intrigued but—naturally—wary about change. The hospital church is so different from anything they've ever seen or done, it throws people for a loop.

I observe this again and again wherever I speak about hospital church style ministry. Whenever I teach the biblical and practical basis for it, people almost universally agree that transition to a hospital church ministry is needed. It's clearly biblical and reflects the character of Jesus. Yet, even with that agreement, many are still unwilling to venture out through the gate and begin.

This frustrated me for some time, but early one morning it dawned on me that I wasn't adequately answering the "why" question for those I taught. Why push through the gate to get to the green grass on the other side? The joy of a result must outweigh the pain of a change—because, yes, pain will be involved in helping facilitate any type of transition in your church. Change is hard work. I won't sugarcoat this for you. Transitioning to a hospital church model will require your time, energy, and resources.

So, before we go any further, I want to point out ten benefits of transitioning to a hospital church ministry in your church. Clearly, if people's lives experience healing and growth, it's an immensely good thing. But what effect will this ministry have upon the church, staff, pastor, and leadership team who help facilitate the change? Why push through the difficulties associated with the transition? Right up front, you need to know that it will be worth it in the end.

Can I have a drum roll, please?

## TOP TEN BENEFITS OF BECOMING A HOSPITAL CHURCH

### #10—*The joy factor explodes*

Simply put, helped people are happy people.

Remember when Jesus healed the blind man in John 9. Plenty of religious folks were upset with that. They wanted to question the man to death, to hang him by his sins. But the man's response showed a bottom-line glee: "One thing I do know. I was blind and now I see!" (John 9:25 NIV).

How beautifully simple is that response? I can imagine this man running through the streets, laughing, shouting, telling people all about his newfound sight. The man's answer has an unrestrained character to it—a raw and naked joy. It has a purity that comes only when people who have long ago given up hope suddenly discover it with a joy and energy never believed possible.

It has been our experience at Celebration Fellowship that people whose lives have been changed bring this same type of joy to our church. Their testimonies often revolve around similar simple and pure messages: "I once was blind but now I see. I may not know anything else, but I know that—and it's a cause for celebration. Let's dance in the streets! Let's give glory to God!"

Would you rather have a church filled with people who seem to have been weaned on dill pickles, or people like the blind man who now can see? A hospital church ministry will fill your church with people who change the temperature and atmosphere of your church. It will turn whining people into winning people!

Give me people who once were blind but now can see any day of the week. That's who I want to hang out with. That's who I want to do life and ministry with.

### #9—More people accept Christ

When people experience healing, it opens their hearts to the message of Jesus Christ in new ways. We love to see people come to know the Lord at our church. Radical conversion experiences are the lifeblood of the body.

Before coming to our church, many of the people were active in twelve-step recovery groups that meet in our surrounding community.[1] They came to the Hospital Church through a relationship with a Hospital Church member who was also a part of the twelve-step group.

Here's the exciting thing: What we have found is that when people get into a twelve-step group for sobriety, they develop a spiritual consciousness that they may have never had before. It's the Higher Power emphasized in that process. Their hearts are opened to spiritual things in new ways. If they get to know Christians who know Jesus Christ, the true higher power, who are also recovering, they see something different

---

1. A crucial part of the ministry of any hospital church is to people recovering from addictions to alcohol, drugs, sex, gambling, food, and the host of other substances and behaviors people become addicted to. However, to be clear, the majority of people we minister to at Celebration Fellowship are not addicts but everyday people who suffer from emotional wounds in their pasts. These wounds cause ongoing difficulties in their lives and relationships. They are people just like you and me. They come from every tax, educational, and social bracket. Some are down and out, but many are up and in. In truth, all of us have wounds at some level.

in those Christians' lives. That opens up a dialogue that leads to either a direct presentation of the gospel or an invitation to a church that embraces recovering people in love and acceptance. Jesus called this being salt and light in the world. We call it the ministry of attraction.

They then come to the Hospital Church and are loved into a relationship with Christ. They also find ministries in the church that take them deeper into recovery than they were experiencing before, as we help them deal with emotional wounds in their lives.

As these people continue to go to their twelve-step group, other recovering addicts see the changes that are happening in their lives, and questions start to be asked. The positive cycle repeats itself over and over. Incidentally, that's why we have never encouraged our recovering people to stop attending their secular twelve-step groups. If all the Christians withdraw from the twelve-step groups that meet in the community, how are we going to make an impact for Christ in those environments?

### #8—*Giving goes up, not down*

I hesitate to talk about money because true ministry is not linked to how much or little of it a church has. However, I mention it because I recognize that church leaders need to be administrators too, and I know leaders often fear that the church's budget will go down the toilet if they begin this kind of ministry. After all, how can destitute people fund the budget of the church?

But that fear is based upon the false assumption that all addicts are destitute and that all emotionally hurting people are down and out. However, addiction and emotional pain know no tax bracket, social strata, or educational accomplishment. Hurting people come from all walks of life. There are plenty of people from all economic positions in our church. We minister to many professionals, business owners, and materially successful people.

I can't make any promises in this area, but I can tell you what our experience has been: Becoming a hospital church has enlarged the finances of Celebration Fellowship.

From 1984 until 1992 (the year we transitioned into a hospital church model), the church never once met the annual budget. There were years when I took a pay cut because finances were so bleak. (I have more annual vacation time now than I can ever take, because back then when they couldn't give me a raise, they would give me another week of vacation!) I was always in the position many pastors find themselves in of trying to convince people to give. I hated it. They hated it. It was never effective except for short periods of time.

From 1992 through the present day, the Hospital Church has overgiven the budget every single year! From 1992 to 2009, we have bought more land and built more buildings, and our budget has grown more than 500 percent. The church has been debt-free for years. In 2009, we completed a 30,000-square-foot children's facility and borrowed only 25 percent of the construction cost. We are paying double payments and intend to be debt-free again in four years. I never preach about giving. I don't need to. We don't do an annual budget campaign with a big push to promote the budget. The elders prepare the budget, we present it to the church, and the people give. They give out of gratitude to God for His mercy in their life.

Someone once said, "Money flows to good ideas." I believe that is true. Our experience has been that money flows to a ministry that provides real, life-changing, caring, and compassionate help. That is the kind of ministry a hospital church facilitates. For the first few years after transitioning to the hospital church model, we didn't connect the dots about what was happening with our church's new, healthier financial situation. Then someone pointed it out, and we all said, "Huh, go figure."

I believe any church that gives itself to this kind of ministry and is a good steward will experience the same thing over time. People want to give when they know it is not just to keep the machine running. They give when they see real life-change happening around them—and in them. That's worth giving to.

### #7—Church health is boosted, not lowered
One of the concerns church leaders often voice to me is, "How can a church be healthy if it's filled with many hurting and recovering people?"

It sounds like a contradiction, but it's true—having a bunch of hurting people in your church is good for your church. When the hurting people are beginning to heal, that is.

Truthfully, every church is filled with just as many hurting people as Celebration Fellowship. Wounded people are always there—whether you see them or not. The difference is that in the Hospital Church they are no longer just hurting or hiding people, but now they are healing people.

At first glance, this style of church ministry might look messier, but in many senses it's simply a more honest way of doing ministry. People aren't hiding their pain anymore; they're dealing with it. Having a hospital church ministry in your church boosts your church's health.

### #6—Conflict and controversy go down

Most people think a hospital church would be a place of chaos. The exact opposite is true.

In a hospital church, people are learning to live by principles that reduce conflict. For instance, one of the core values of the recovery process is to accept personal responsibility in any problem. It's what Jesus said about dealing with the log in your own eye before you worry about the speck of dust in someone else's (Matt. 7:5). We call it "keeping your own side of the street clean."

Where people learn to take responsibility, there is far less finger pointing and less conflict. And when there is conflict, it is resolved more quickly. When people's focus is on growing and helping others to grow, mature, and heal, they don't have nearly as much energy for backbiting, gossip, and trying to control others.

This doesn't mean that there is never any conflict or controversy. We have had our share at Celebration Fellowship and undoubtedly will have more in the future. But what we have discovered is that the conflict and controversy is almost always started or fueled by people who are not participating in the healing ministry that forms the core of the church, or people who have deviated from those principles. We have people who are a part of our church because they believe in the ministry but were not willing to get involved themselves in the process of emotional healing. More often than not, these are the same people who are in the middle of trouble when it happens. We have discovered that if we are relentless about moving people into the healing process and keeping them there, not only will they be blessed, but the church at large is also blessed.

### #5—Loyalty goes up

The proverbial back door is a problem every church faces. It's a fact of life in a fast paced, changing, and transitional culture. People come and go for many reasons. No church will be able to close the back door completely because of the nature of the culture in which we live. However, some of the things that propel people toward that back door can be addressed.

"There is nothing here that meets my needs" was something I heard for years from people as they left the church, and I hated it every time I heard it. In the Hospital Church, we are far from perfect. We have made mistakes by the truckloads and have had people come in the front door and go out the back. But we have grown—and are still growing—in understanding how to address this complaint.

Along the way we have discovered that if people genuinely get involved in the process of growth and healing, then they rarely leave. They are far more willing to hash out differences and misunderstandings, because they'd rather do that than leave the relationships that have helped them grow and mature.

This kind of loyalty is vital to the ongoing life of a hospital church because those people are needed for the continued growth and expansion of the ministry, just as they are in any church.

In business, high employee turnover is very costly. After a company has invested the resources of time and money to train and educate an employee, the worst thing that can happen is for the employee to leave. All the investment is wasted and must be repeated.

The same is true in ministry. After we have invested time and resources into people's lives, it is devastating for them to leave just when they are ready to become productive in the ministry to others. Let me say it again. Sometimes people do leave our church. Sometimes they even leave mad! But it is very rare that someone who is really engaged in the process goes out the back door.

### #4—Relationships deepen

One of the keys to the growth of any church, and to the growth of individuals within it, is relationships. When people don't develop relationships, they don't grow, and they usually don't stay. Keys elements to developing relationships are openness, honesty, and transparency.

The heart of the Hospital Church work is accomplished in small groups called freedom groups. These groups are all about honesty and transparency. Once a week, for twelve to fourteen weeks, people gather to share their pasts, fears, hurts, failures, and victories. They encourage and pray for one another. They develop bonds in that process that last.

Because the Hospital Church offers many different types of freedom groups, most of our people have been in several groups. Eventually some go on to become the facilitator of a freedom group. With each group experience they are broadening their web of intimate relationships. Within their groups are people they have shared with, grown with, and sometimes cried with. People get to know each other beyond a handshake and cup of coffee in the foyer on Sunday mornings. In a Bible study class or a traditional small group, people get to know one another and develop friendships—that's a good thing. Yet, in a freedom group, people develop intimacy—that's the best thing. The bonds of intimacy are not easily broken.

### #3—It's the true answer to "WWJD?"

Any time you read the Gospels, you discover who Jesus spent the majority of His time with. Christ gravitated toward the hurting, the outcast, and the sinner. He spent so much time with these types of people that the religious leaders turned it against him. Jesus' tongue-in-cheek response was, "It is the sick who need a physician, not the well" (see Luke 5:31). The truth was that Jesus knew the Pharisees were just as sick as anyone

He ministered to. They just lived in denial of their sickness and need (cf. Matt. 23:25–28)

What would Jesus do? He cares for sick and hurting people. When a church becomes a place where the Great Physician can do His work, it will reflect the very heart of Christ.

### #2—It gives a church a clear purpose

A few years ago, I met with some leaders of a church that was on its last leg. They were talking about coming on board with our church. I spent several hours with them casting the vision of hospital church ministry. At the end of the time, one of the seasoned leaders of that church said, "It's so wonderful to hear about a church that has a clear vision for what they are doing. We haven't had a clear vision for so long that I can't even remember what the vision originally was."

That statement reflects the main reason that church was on the road to oblivion. No vision. No direction. Just meeting and going through the motions.

If a church locks into hospital church ministry, it will give that church a vision that is big enough, caring enough, compassionate enough, and worthy enough for people to give their lives to. That explains why people in the Hospital Church give so sacrificially of their time and lives. The vision compels. The help, hope, and healing they have received, and the vision of helping others to find hope, help, and healing in Christ, is big enough to give their lives to.

### #1—It reduces the counseling load of the pastor and staff

If you're a pastor today, you just breathed a sigh of relief reading reason #1 above. Today's pastors have tremendous demands placed upon their time and lives. Anything that would add to the counseling load would be too much.

I know what it's like to be the go-to guy for counseling. I used to feel like I was a big extension cord with multiple inputs. Every time I walked by someone, they plugged into me and drained more energy and life out of me. I don't feel that way anymore.

Many pastors have the wrong perception that a hospital church ministry would increase their load. The exact opposite is true. For a hospital church ministry to be effective, the people need to accomplish it. People minister to each other. It happens in the freedom group structure and in one-on-one mentoring. It's the purest expression of body life I have ever experienced. Over time, the pastor and staff are involved less and less in the hands-on counseling and mentoring. They are freed up to equip, train, and administrate the ministry of the church. They get to have lives of their own.

When someone comes to see me with a crisis in their marriage or a problem with addiction or emotional pain, I don't take them on as a long-term counseling project. I get them connected with a freedom group. Sometimes I pick up the phone and call one of the people on my long list of persons who have given me permission to call them any time there is someone who needs help. These are people who have been helped and are willing to help others. They do it willingly and gladly! They consider it a privilege to give back the help and encouragement they once received. And they are able to relate closely with this person's struggle because they have been there themselves.

Having a hospital church ministry decreases the pastors' counseling load by increasing the service base of the church. People who find, in Christ, new life and freedom from wounds and addictions develop huge servant hearts. They learn that part of their continued growth and healing is dependent upon helping others as they have been helped. Jesus said, "As you have freely received, freely give" (see Matt. 10:8).

Pastor, church leader, layperson, do yourself a favor. Build a hospital church and you will be surrounded by a cadre of people who will do the work more effectively than you could ever dream of doing it alone.

## A CHURCH FOR YOU

Open your mind and allow yourself to think outside of your ministry box, to embrace a different paradigm. I believe that you will be blessed, your church will be blessed, and the lives of people you work with will be blessed. That has been my experience. I believe it can be yours too.

And I believe the heart of Jesus will be blessed when He sees His body, the church, continuing the kind of work He started while He was on earth in bodily form.

# PART THREE

# The Basis

CHAPTER 4

# THE EMOTIONAL-SPIRITUAL PRINCIPLE

Some time ago, a forty-four-year-old man approached our church looking for help and counsel. I'll call him Ron. He said he was a Christ follower and frequently attended another church, but he had heard we were helping people make real breakthroughs in their lives. He was curious as to how. He made frequent references to Scripture in his talk. I believe he was genuine in his faith.

Ron's problem was a recurring pattern of involvement with women, usually married women, in relationships that honored neither God, himself, nor the woman. Ron was frustrated with his repeated sinful and destructive choices.

As we talked further, Ron spoke about being raised in a loveless home. He recognized how this experience had fostered within him an unhealthy need that kept drawing him into sin. He just didn't know how to break the cycle. Each time this pattern repeated itself, Ron experienced remorse and confession of his sin. Eventually it would happen all over again.

Ron's story is not uncommon in pastoral ministry. Many people genuinely desire to have intimate and growing relationships with God, but they're stuck in destructive patterns. And for every person willing to risk admitting to a struggle, there are so many more who never do. Many people live their lives with destructive secrets and patterns until their lives eventually implode or explode. It happens in churches all the time. People who seem to have it all together aren't going forward in their faith. Or they suddenly fall apart. Or they're stuck in destructive behaviors. Or their marriage breaks up. Or they drift from their faith. Or they quit positions of service or leadership. Or they leave church in a huff. Or, often, they just go away quietly and we never hear from or see them again.

Ron's story is the story of you, me, and everyone who's ever experienced a problem and gone to a church for help. His struggle—and knowing how to help him with it—is what this book is about. More specifically, it is what this chapter is about.

How would you respond today if Ron came to you for help? Send him back to his own church? Refer him to outside counseling? Recommend that he join a small group? Prescribe more spiritual disciplines such as prayer and Bible reading? Tell him to read a book?

As I look back over my own years of pastoral ministry, I am saddened by the anemic, inept, sometimes trite, and often ineffective answers I gave to so many people before I understood what twenty-five years of sitting in a pew can do.

Simply put: it's not enough. Much of what we've done in church doesn't work. And our old methods of helping people are becoming increasingly ineffective. We've missed one important truth—and that truth often sounds like the exact opposite of what we have been taught or ever understood.

## A COUNTERINTUITIVE TRUTH

Over the years, I have spoken about this missing truth and have met with varied responses. Some people immediately embrace the teaching and find in it answers to questions that they have struggled with for years. Others wrestle with it, argue about it, and then reject it outright. For some, it just doesn't sound spiritual enough. So I introduce this principle here in full recognition of its controversial nature. It is not controversial because it is contrary to Scripture but because it is counterintuitive. It's not something many have ever been taught in church or seminary. During thirty-seven years in the faith and a total of eleven years of professional training for ministry through college and seminary, I never heard it taught. Yet it is firmly rooted in Scripture.

The controversial, counterintuitive truth is this: You can never be more spiritually mature than you are emotionally mature. This principle, which I call the emotional-spiritual principle, can be expressed in several ways:

- Your spiritual growth will never go beyond your emotional growth.

- You can never have a more intimate relationship with God than you are capable of having with other people.

- Your level of emotional maturity will always create a ceiling for your spiritual maturity.

All of these statements communicate the same truth. It's what Ron needed to grasp to break his destructive lifestyle patterns and before he could go forward in his spiritual walk. There is an unbreakable link between emotional and spiritual health. You can't have one without the other.

God has created us as both emotional and spiritual beings, and these two facets of our being are intricately linked according to His design. Addressing only one will always result in the achievement of less than our full potential in Christ.

I've seen this emotional-spiritual principle at work. Often, people who have been Christians for many years, studied the Bible extensively, and even been involved in Christian service, will become involved in a freedom group process designed for addressing emotional wounds. They begin to experience emotional healing and find that their spiritual maturity moves to levels they have never known before. Sometimes, six months to a year later they will say, "I have been a Christian for thirty years, but I have grown more in my relationship with Christ in the past year than all those thirty years combined. Why is this happening? I don't understand it!"

The answer is that they've raised the emotional ceiling. The emotional blocks to spiritual maturity are being removed. And when a child of God begins this process, the sky's the limit for what can happen in their relationships to other people and in their relationship to God.

Let's unpack this idea more in depth.

## THE GUTS OF SPIRITUAL MATURITY

When most Christians are asked to define spiritual maturity their response typically revolves around the traditional disciplines of the Christian life. They say something like, "A mature Christian is someone who studies and knows the Bible, prays, serves, gives, and is regular in worship attendance." In other words, we usually define spiritual maturity by certain faith-based activities that hopefully connect us with God.

Please don't misunderstand me—the disciplines are all important aspects of the mature Christian life, and any mature Christian should demonstrate these on a consistent level in sincerity of heart. But they are not by themselves sure indicators of spiritual maturity. Nor are they surefire cure-alls for every person's malady. Think about it: sometimes people who are very spiritually immature can possess volumes of Bible knowledge, pray for extended periods of time, and be in church every time the doors are open. Spiritually immature people can tithe, fast, give, and be actively involved in every aspect of the local church, even leadership. That's why I say that a lifetime of sitting in a pew simply doesn't cut it. The spiritual disciplines themselves do not define spiritual maturity.

Let me be clear: there is outright danger in using the Christian disciplines as guaranteed indicators of spiritual maturity. For years I made this mistake. When someone came to me expressing a desire to grow in spiritual maturity, I would immediately direct them to the Christian disciplines as the answer. In essence I was telling them that the way to spiritual maturity was to *do* more—give more, pray more, study more, serve more. The Pharisees did all of these things, yet Jesus repeatedly told them that they had no connection to the Father because their hearts were far from God (see Matt. 15:1–9). They were accomplished in the disciplines but were hardly spiritually mature.

The word *mature* indicates someone or something that has enlarged in its capacity. An oak tree matures from a sapling into a fully grown tree. The human body matures from a 7-pound newborn into a 180-pound man. Maturity speaks of increased capacity. A mature tree has more capacity to give shade, bear fruit, or be cut down for lumber. A mature man has more capacity to talk, work, think, eat, and do any of the other hundreds of activities that mature humans are called to do. So when we are speaking of spiritual maturity, we are talking about an enlarged capacity. We have to ask: enlarged capacity for what? The answer is for an intimate relationship with the Father. Spiritual maturity isn't primarily about knowledge, activity, or even service. It is about a growing capacity for an intimate, loving relationship with God.

When Jesus was asked what the greatest commandment was, He shocked His hearers with His response: "'Love the Lord your God with all your heart, and with all your soul, and with all your mind.' This is the greatest and foremost commandment. The second is like it, 'You shall love your neighbor as yourself'" (Matt. 22:37–39). He said the Law and the Prophets depended upon these two factors (v. 40). Without these two foundational stones in place, all the rest of the spiritual building comes crumbling down. All of the prayer, fasting, studying, giving, serving becomes empty, meaningless, ritual behavior unless loving God and loving others is in place. The most important thing of all is the capacity to have an intimate love relationship with the Father and with other people. Few Christians would have a problem with this teaching. It's the second part of the Great Commandment—loving others—that often stymies well-intentioned believers.

## THE GUTS OF EMOTIONAL MATURITY

Emotional maturity is not about being able to express emotions. Sometimes emotionally immature people can be very adept at expressing their emotions. They express them all over the place. But can they connect with others on an intimate level, soul to soul? Can they correctly identify and express their emotions to love and be loved, as Christ commanded? The answers to these questions point to whether someone is emotionally mature or not. Emotional maturity is an increased capacity for intimacy with other people. A lack of emotional maturity hinders our ability to maintain long-term, intimate, human relationships.

The operative word here is "intimate." A dictionary defines intimate as "belonging to or characterizing one's deepest nature."[1] An intimate relationship goes beyond the surface and penetrates to the very deepest part of the human soul. The length of a relationship is not always an indication of its intimacy, because people sometimes hold on to relationships out of stubbornness, the refusal to give up, or from ignorance that anything more is available. Comedian Rodney Dangerfield once quipped, "My wife and I eat our meals at different times, we sleep in different rooms, and take separate vacations. Hey—we're doing everything we can to keep this marriage together!" That's so sad it's funny—yet it shows the epitome of emotional immaturity in practice, the inability to truly connect with others.

Where does this inability come from?

We live in a sinful world. As we move through this fallen world, hurtful and damaging things happen to us. None of us completely escapes the experiences that create emotional wounds. These wounds may vary in severity from person to person—from the very deep and devastating for some, to more superficial for others. Yet at some level we have all been wounded, and we all need some measure of emotional healing. In this world there are none who have escaped the effects of the fall. Most of our wounds come from:

- Harmful things said to (or about) us
- Destructive things done to us
- Good things taken from us

---

1. *Merriam-Webster's Collegiate Dictionary*, 11th edition, s.v., "intimate."

These wounds cumulate in unmet desires—things people take from us or fail to give us that we believe we deserve. Sometimes the wounds even come from destructive or harmful things we do to ourselves, often in response to something painful that initially happened to us.

I'll talk about the sources of wounding in more depth in the next chapter. But it's safe to say that, because of these wounds, a person might be forty years of age but have the capacity for intimate human relationships of only a twelve-year-old. He may look successful in business or be a leader in the church. She may in many ways appear to be a confident, self-possessed, and mature adult. But when you look closely, this man or woman is extremely wounded, guarded, defensive, or depressed. This person is incapable of truly connecting intimately with others . . . and, ultimately, with God.

Emotionally wounding experiences tend to create fear, anger, mistrust, bitterness, resentment, and a lack of forgiveness. All of these things hamper people from developing intimate human relationships. They cause people to go through life with elbows that don't bend all the way. We will allow people to get only so close, and then we'll begin to hold them off. To refer back to *Webster's* definition of intimacy, we are afraid to let others know us at our "deepest nature."

I refer to this emotional guardedness as the "Heisman pose." (For any non-football fans, the Heisman Trophy is given out annually to the most outstanding college football player in the United States. The statue shows a player carrying a football beneath one arm, with his other arm outstretched in a classic stiff-arm position, the standard technique for a ball-carrier to push potential tacklers away.) Emotionally wounded people go through life in the Heisman pose, stiff-arming others away, incapable, or unwilling, to risk allowing others to get too close. This stiff-arm behavior becomes so ingrained as a way of doing life that with time the individual may no longer even be aware it is happening.

For most of my life I was stuck in the Heisman pose. As an emotionally wounded person, emotional intimacy was too great a risk, so I kept people at a safe distance from me. Even when I found myself longing for deeper intimacy with others I couldn't achieve it. I simply didn't know how. This emotional immaturity stunted my ability to connect with God as well. And I had no idea how to connect deeply with anyone—God or otherwise. I needed to discover the principle of emotional-spiritual health. It's taught all through Scripture. Somehow I had missed it.

## ROOTED IN SCRIPTURE

My wife and I have two grown children, three years apart in age. When my children were small, whenever they got along with each other and treated one another with kindness, it made the entire family atmosphere more open and unhindered. The sky was a little brighter, everyone's spirit was a little lighter, even the pizza tasted better. As their father, I was free to express my connection to them on a deep, intimate level.

But when my kids weren't getting along, the atmosphere was altogether different. When one of them was being mean or hurtful to the other, the whole family felt it. As a parent, I found that it even caused a hindrance to my sense of closeness to each child. It didn't mean that I didn't love the child. But it meant that my free-flowing expression of love, and the sense of close connection, was hindered because of the problem between brother and sister.

My wife and I realized this connection—between how our kids got along and how we were able to relate to them—so deeply that we established a family principle about it: Treating each other with anything less than dignity and respect was simply not acceptable in our home. Our kids weren't perfect, and con-flicts inevitably happened. But when they did, the issues were immediately addressed, apologies tendered, and hugs given. That practice promoted an atmosphere where true relational in-timacy could blossom. Wounds from hurts were not allowed to fester and poison relationships.

The same principle holds true with our spiritual families: How we relate to one another as siblings in the family of God affects the atmosphere of the entire family and our expression of intimacy with the Father. Matthew 5:23–24 talks about a man at an altar giving an offering to God. Then he remembers a fractured relationship with a brother. Jesus instructs anyone in this kind of situation to leave his offering at the altar, go and first be reconciled to the brother, then come back and present the offering. Jesus clearly establishes the close connection between how we relate to one another and how we relate with God. The modern-day equivalent of this passage would be an instruction to leave church if there comes to mind a broken relationship that you have refused to deal with. Stop the praise songs, stop the prayers, stop the offering plate, and climb over the chairs if you have to. Go get right, then come back and worship. There is a clear connection between the vertical relationship (to the Father) and the horizontal (to one another).

Let's take a look at a few more passages that show the emotional-spiritual principle at work: In Matthew 5:7, Jesus says, "Blessed are the merciful, for they shall receive mercy." This verse indicates that our experience of God's mercy will be tempered by our expression of mercy toward others. If we give mercy, we will get it in return. Again, our relationship with God is affected by our relationship with others.

Similarly, one of the requests in the Lord's Prayer is that God would "forgive us our debts, as we also have forgiven our debtors" (Matt. 6:13). There are two ways to look at this request. On the one hand, if we have forgiven others, then we are asking God to forgive us. On the other, if we are harboring unforgiveness, this prayer is a request that the Father limit our experience of the fullness of His forgiveness! If we are to pray for forgiveness on the same basis that we are willing to forgive, then both perspectives are true.

It is God's desire to forgive and He does so when we genuinely ask Him (see 1 John 1:9). But it is also His desire that we walk in the fullness of the experience of His forgiveness. Christ indicated that our ability to live in that fullness, and experience the full freedom of His forgiveness, is limited at some level by our unwillingness, or inability, to forgive others. In Matthew 6:14–15,

Jesus says, "For if you forgive others for their transgressions, your heavenly Father will also forgive you. But if you do not forgive others, then your Father will not forgive your transgressions." This passage clearly makes the connection between our horizontal relationship with others and our vertical relationship with the Father.

A similar teaching in Matthew 25:35–40 shows us that one way we serve Christ is by serving others in His name. Jesus speaks of what He will say to those who are invited into His presence, "For I was hungry, and you gave Me something to eat; I was thirsty, and you gave Me something to drink; I was a stranger, and you invited me in. . . ."

To which some of the crowd it seems will respond: When did we do those things for you, Lord?

Jesus will respond: "To the extent that you did it to one of these brothers of Mine, even the least of them, you did it to Me" (v. 40). Jesus is saying that our relationship to Him cannot be separated from our relationship to others. Once again, the connection is clear that how we relate to Him is intricately linked with how we relate to others.

First Peter 3:7 warns husbands to "live with your wives in an understanding way . . . so that your prayers may not be hindered." God's ear to a husband's prayer is affected by the honor that he gives to—or withholds from—his wife.

Loving each other and loving God are two primary themes throughout the book of 1 John. "If someone says, 'I love God,' and hates his brother, he is a liar; for the one who does not love his brother whom he has seen, cannot love God whom he has not seen" (4:20). In other words, the love of one's brother cannot be separated from the love of one's God. In the second half of this verse, John even says that our ability to love God is affected by our ability to love our brother.

Paul wrote to the church in Corinth to address problems within the church. In 1 Corinthians 3, he addresses their spiritual immaturity: "And I, brethren, could not speak to you as to spiritual men, but as to men of flesh, as to infants in Christ. I gave you milk to drink, not solid food; for you were not yet able to receive it. Indeed even now you are not yet able" (vv. 1–2).

In the next verse he gives the evidence of their spiritual immaturity when he says, "for you are still fleshly. For since there is jealousy and strife among you, are you not fleshly, and are you not walking like mere men?" (v. 3). It could be said that the strife and jealousy among them was both the evidence of their spiritual immaturity and the cause of it. Either way, Paul indicated the connection between their spiritual maturity and the way they related to one another.

## A LOVE THAT NEEDS DEFINING

The emotional-spiritual principle states that you can't have a more intimate relationship with God than you are capable of having with other people. Within this principle is the directive to love yourself. Jesus said it directly in the Great Commandment: "love your neighbor *as yourself*" (Matt. 22:39, emphasis added).

I realize that anytime someone talks about self-love, that person is walking on treacherous ground. There is much out there about self-love that widely misses the mark of what God intends. Much of what is said is shot through with humanistic philosophy and results in a worship of self, rather than in a release to love others and love God more completely. A humanistic-styled self-love where you tell yourself how good you are, how worthy you are, how valuable you are, is not what I'm talking about.

Biblical self-love is simply seeing ourselves as God sees us—through the imputed righteousness of Christ. It is accepting our true identity in Christ and becoming secure in who we are because of Christ's work on the cross.[2] Insecurity, a lack of healthy love for self, is perhaps the greatest form of pride and self-centeredness because it prevents me from loving others and caring about others. You see, insecurity focuses the attention on me. Insecurity causes me to go through life with my surface-to-air radar on all the time looking for missiles that someone is going

---

2. See Robert McGee, *Search for Significance* (Nashville: Thomas Nelson, 2003).

to fire at me. I'm constantly searching for the hidden message in what you say or don't say. When I'm insecure, I'm constantly on the defensive; my fight-or-flight mechanism never shuts down. This destroys marriages, friendships, working relationships, and churches. Insecurity kills our relationships with others and with our God.

To illustrate this, imagine with me a beautiful landscape. Think of the most beautiful scene you have ever seen. For me, it would be several years ago when I stood on a cliff top on the island of Maui with a beautiful view of the aqua blue waters of the Pacific Ocean below. The cliff top formed a plateau of beautiful green grass, mature trees, and patches of beautiful flowers.

Let's picture ourselves walking along through the beauty. But as we walk, we don't see any of it. We don't see the sparkling water, the rippling grass, the massive trees, or the exotic flowers. Why? Because in our mind we secretly believe the scenic cliff top is laced with landmines. As we walk through this beautiful scene, all of our focus, energy, and attention are used in searching at our feet for what will harm us. We're afraid that at any minute our legs will get blown off—or worse.

But there is no minefield. The only mines are the ones we have created in our mind. An imaginary threat causes us to completely miss the beauty of the scene.

That is what insecurity does to us in life. God has put us on earth and surrounded us with the beauty of human relationships and a relationship with Him through Christ, but because of emotional woundedness and insecurity we may miss it all. This is insecurity: protecting ourselves from threats that aren't even there. We miss the beauty of all of those relationships because our focus is on ourselves.

So what is the pathway out of this insecurity trap? It's found in Jesus' command to love others as we love ourselves. Real love in any direction is a miracle of God. An ability to really love myself, others, and God in the way that He wants me to is not something I can generate within myself. If God is love, and the Scripture says He is (1 John 4:8), then the kind of love that Jesus is talking about can come only from

Him. Any love I try to muster on my own is a lousy substitute for the real thing. Christ has to teach us how to love and empower us in this way.

Everything about emotional healing is designed to move me out of the insecure self-centeredness that emotional woundedness creates in me. It is designed to free me to love myself, love others, and love God. God wants to bring healing to my wounds so that I can be released to love in all three directions in a way that honors Him and promotes His purpose in my life and the lives of others around me. It's all about Him, not me.

## THE EMOTIONAL/SPIRITUAL CIRCLE

Six biblical words sum up the work of the Hospital Church as it relates to the process of emotional healing: grace, faith, peace, love, fellowship, and worship. Emotional healing comes through

> learning to live by Grace
>     through faith,
>
> which results in personal peace,
>     love of others,
>     fellowship,
>
> and, ultimately, genuine and unhindered worship.

Let's unpack that word by word.

### Grace: Accepted by God

Grace is God accepting me in Christ. Grace means I don't deserve His acceptance, and I can't earn His acceptance—I get His acceptance as a free gift. Grace means He accepts me not because of who I am or what I can do but because of who Christ is and what Christ has done for me on the cross. He doesn't love me because I am valuable. I have value because He loves me. My worth and value are determined by His Grace.

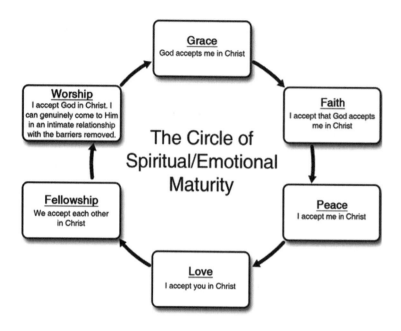

Ephesians 2:8 says, "For by grace you have been saved. . . ." Saved from what? Everything! Saved from the eternal penalty of my sin. Saved from my separation from God. Saved from having only the power of my human flesh to make life work. Saved—what a wonderful word. "In Christ" I am accepted by God. That's grace.

### Faith: How I receive Grace

Faith is me accepting the acceptance God offers me in Christ. Ephesians 2:8 goes on to say, "For by grace you have been saved *through faith. . .*" (emphasis added). Faith at its essence is taking God at His Word. It's believing that Christ has paid the eternal penalty for my sin on the cross, and if I will turn to Christ as Savior and submit myself to Him then God will apply that payment to my life and free me from the penalty of eternal death. That is when I receive the free gift of salvation. When I take God at His Word and do as He has commanded in trusting Christ as Savior, that's faith. Faith is the channel through which I receive grace.

Faith doesn't stop at salvation. We have to go on and live our lives in Christ by faith. Romans 1:17 says, "the just shall live by faith" (NKJV). This is where many of us blow it. We accept that God accepts us in Christ for salvation, but then we don't live in the freedom of His acceptance in our daily lives. Instead, we launch out on our daily struggle to earn His acceptance, never really believing that we have it. We feel that God doesn't really accept us, so we can't accept ourselves or others. That's insecurity.

Security comes when I begin to live by grace through faith every day. When I take God at His Word—that I am accepted by Him in Christ—then I can begin to love myself, others, and God.

Then, the first result of living by grace through faith is peace.

### Peace: The Result of Security in Christ

When God accepts me in Christ, and I accept that He accepts me in Christ, then I can accept myself in Christ and the result is inner peace in Christ. The struggle to earn His acceptance ends, and I begin to live in the peace of who I am in Christ. The inner turmoil of insecurity begins to calm, and there is peace. Philippians 4:7 says, "The peace of God, which surpasses all comprehension, will guard your hearts and your minds in Christ Jesus." Where is this peace? It's in Christ Jesus. Healing can happen only *in Christ*. Every other path falls far short of the mark of what God intends. Every other attempt is a cheap substitute. When I begin to experience this inner peace as a result of living by grace through faith it releases me to the next step of emotional healing.

### Love: The ability to accept others in Christ

When God accepts me in Christ, and I accept that He accepts me in Christ, and I begin to experience the inner peace of that acceptance, then it frees me to begin to accept others. I'm able to love others the way God intends for me to love them. I don't have to see others as a threat anymore. I can drop my protective guard. I can take my eyes off myself and begin to truly look at others and love them.

Jesus said to His disciples on His last night with them, "A new commandment I give to you, that you love one another, even as I have loved you, that you also love one another. By this all men will know that you are My disciples, if you have love for one another" (John 13:34–35). The love we are to have for each other is to be so radically different that even unbelievers will recognize that something miraculous is taking place. People in the world just don't love like this. True love is possible only *in Christ.*

Now, this is when it really gets exciting in the Hospital Church: when people begin to experience the healing of the emotional wounds that have sabotaged their love of self, love of others, and love of God and start loving others as Christ commanded. When people in Christ do this together it results in the next piece of emotional healing.

### Fellowship: The beautiful result

When God accepts me in Christ (grace), and I accept that I am accepted by God in Christ (faith), and I accept myself in Christ and have the inner peace that results from that acceptance (peace), then I can begin to accept others in Christ (love). And if that same process is working in you, then you can begin to truly love me, and we have true fellowship together. Biblical fellowship is where people are living by grace through faith, and by the peace and love that are released by that grace and faith.

First John 1:6–7 says, "If we say that we have fellowship with Him and yet walk in the darkness, we lie and do not practice the truth; but if we walk in the Light as He Himself is in the Light, we have fellowship with one another, and the blood of Jesus His Son cleanses us from all sin." So, fellowship is all because of our being *in Christ.* In fact, it is only fully possible *in Christ.*

Jesus gave us a command in John 13:34 that is humanly impossible to obey. It is not within us to love one another as He has loved us. If it happens, when it happens, it comes from Him. It's His love, not ours. He has to create it in us; He has to do it through us. It's all by grace through faith.

*Worship: The ultimate goal*
When I am moving through each step around this circle I am removing blocks to unhindered worship of God. This is true intimacy. This is true growth in spiritual maturity. This isn't a one-time trip. It's a process for an entire life. Each time I go around this circle I discover new depths of what it means to be accepted in Christ, to accept that I am accepted in Christ, and so on. This is the process of emotional/spiritual growth. This is the process of being transformed (Rom. 12:2).

IT CAN BE DONE
When people such as Ron (the man mentioned at the start of this chapter) come to us for advice and counsel, our goal as leaders is to develop them into fully devoted followers of Christ. We want them to be men and women who are spiritually mature, to have an increased capacity for an intimate love relationship with the Father. As such, we must be willing to address anything that stands in the way of that relationship growing to its desired capacity.
Now let me summarize what I've presented about the emotional-spiritual principle:

• Scripture clearly establishes the case that anything that hinders our ability to relate to one another in a loving, forgiving, merciful, serving, trusting, and honoring kind of relationship will limit our ability to relate to the Father (see Matt. 5:7, 23–24; 6:12, 14–15; 25:35–40; 1 Peter 3:7; 1 John 4:20).

• We all have emotional wounds because of the fall.

• Emotional wounds create emotional issues such as insecurity, fear, resentment, mistrust, anger, bitterness, and a lack of forgiveness. These issues hinder our ability to relate to ourselves and others in the way that the Father desires.

• When we help people experience emotional healing, we help them overcome their insecurity and fear, release their resentment, and learn to truly forgive others. This opens the way for them to grow in emotional maturity.

- As people travel the path to emotional maturity, they begin experiencing lasting, intimate relationships with themselves and others.

- And this opens the way for them to grow in spiritual maturity, which is having increased capacity for an intimate love relationship to the Father. By helping people experience emotional healing, the ceiling gets raised on true spiritual growth. Hindrances to spiritual intimacy with the Father are removed.

Across the years, as the pastor of a hospital church, I have seen so many illustrations of the emotional-spiritual principle fleshed out in real lives. Ron was one example. We were able to journey with him through this process, and he was able to make the connection between emotional and spiritual health. He's doing much better today.

As another example, I recently had an appointment with a young man in his mid-twenties. He and his wife had been members of the church for six months or so. In that time I had had several discussions with him about his struggle with faith. He was raised in church and came to understand his need for a Savior as a teenager. I would describe him as above-average in his knowledge of Scripture and in his pursuit of an understanding of the things of God. For instance, he reads literature that is apologetic in nature (that deals with the evidences for our faith). He consistently reads the Bible and prays. He and his wife attend church every Sunday, and they attend a Bible study class together.

This young man is desperately seeking to have an intimate connection with God, yet, by his own admission, he does not seem to be getting anywhere. He hears others speak about intimacy with the Father, but he admits he doesn't know what that is like.

In the course of our conversations, we discussed the nature of faith, the character of God, and the testimony of Scripture that God desires an intimate relationship with him. Then I said something that shocked him initially: "For a while, why don't you try putting this pursuit of a relationship with God aside? Just quit trying to figure it all out intellectually and back up a little."

"What do you mean?" he said.

For the next thirty minutes or so I explained to him the principles of the emotional-spiritual connection. As we talked, it became evident to me that this young man was dissatisfied, not only with his relationship with God but with every relationship in his life. He was dissatisfied with his relationship to his career, to his wife, to his family of origin, and to himself.

I suggested to him the possibility that his inability to sense an intimate connection with God was intricately related to his inability to connect on a soul-to-soul level with himself and others in his life. I explained to him that as healing and growth took place at the emotional level and he began to experience a deeper ability to experience soul-to-soul relationships with self and others, the ceiling could be raised for him to experience a greater capacity for a spirit-to-Spirit intimacy with the Father. We laid out a plan of involvement in a safe, accepting, freedom group structure, one where he could tell his secrets and apply biblical principles of healing to his emotional wounds. A place where he could begin to deal with that emotional garbage that had sabotaged his ability to relate on an intimate level not only with other people but also with God.

He left our meeting with hope. The jury is still out on what he will do with the information I gave him. Yet, that's okay. I know that information alone won't bring change. Real change is a process that happens over time. I sense that he is going to take that information and do something with it.[3] As this man left my office, I couldn't keep from giving thanks to God for an un-

---

3. Since this writing, the young man did begin the process, as did his wife. The result has been steady growth, both individually and in their marriage.

derstanding of the emotional-spiritual connection. I also gave thanks for being a part of a church where I have full confidence that this man will have a safe, nurturing environment for the healing journey that he is about to begin. Within this church I have a long list of people I can call on who are also in the process, who will come alongside him, encourage him, and share with him their own stories of change and hope.

It's possible to create such an environment in your church as well. It begins with understanding that a person's level of emotional maturity will always create a ceiling for his or her spiritual maturity, and that the way for a person to have an increased capacity for an intimate relationship with God is through emotional healing.

That's the key.

# CHAPTER 5

# THE PILE PRINCIPLE

In the summer of 2005, my son was scheduled to play in a golf tournament in Myrtle Beach, South Carolina—and I was to be his caddy. I put him on a plane so that he wouldn't have to play competitive golf after a twenty-hour drive in the car. Then, to save a buck, I jumped in my car and headed east, timing my trip so I'd arrive in Myrtle Beach about the same time my son's plane landed.

As I barreled down Interstate 20 that day, I spotted a big, stinking heap of garbage by the side of the road. It all zipped by in a flash, but it looked rotting and revolting, and, strangely enough, the sight prompted a variety of truths to surface in my mind. I had been mulling on these truths for years in a sort of jumbled form, but something about seeing that pile of garbage made them merge together as one. I pulled out a notebook from behind my car seat and began to scribble down thoughts as they came, while steering with my leg. I suppose I should have pulled over, but the thoughts were flying at me so fast I was afraid I'd lose inspiration if I stopped. Thank goodness for cruise control.

What formed in my mind that day was something I named in honor of that big pile of roadside garbage. I grandiosely call it the "Pile Principle." It's a fairly straightforward principle, intrinsically, and it states: "The pile of emotional garbage that we carry through our lives is what sabotages our relationships with God and others."

People sometimes use the term "emotional baggage" to describe much of what I'm about to talk about with the Pile Principle. But, in my mind, the imagery of helping people open their bags and empty them out has always left something to be desired. A suitcase seems too nice, too sanitary, too folded and pressed. Conversely, garbage is repulsive and smelly and putrid, nothing you want hanging around your house for any length of time. A big pile of garbage is all slimed up with eggshells and cold coffee grounds and that moldy casserole you found lurking in the back of your fridge. You're pressed to get rid of it as quickly and thoroughly as possible.

Beyond providing a more relevant mental image, what makes the Pile Principle work for me in describing emotional woundedness are the five biblical truths that progress logically and sequentially from the extended metaphor of a pile of garbage. These five truths were what I was scrambling to write down that day in the car as they unfolded at seventy miles an hour. In the Hospital Church, we have found these truths extremely helpful in bringing people to an understanding of their need to deal with emotional wounds in their life. The Pile Principle has also been useful for many people in understanding why they do destructive things or why their relationships never seem to work very well.

Dealing with the Pile Principle is a key part of the business we're truly in as leaders in the church of helping people move from brokenness to wholeness, immaturity to maturity. People spend years of their life striving and straining to be Spirit-led and heavenly minded, all the while wondering why they're trying so hard only to end up in exactly the same spot. The five truths of the Pile Principle are foundational in helping people get unstuck. These truths challenge people to take responsibility, to invite Christ to help them break the cycle of spiritual futility and to do the hard work of taking their garbage to the curb once and for all. In the process, they discover a spiritual life that is authentic, intimate, often challenging, and anything but boring.

***Truth #1: Everybody has a pile.***

Our piles of emotional garbage come in all sizes and shapes, and from all kinds of sources, but one thing is certain: we all have a pile. None of us walk through this fallen world without collecting some amount of emotional garbage. We are fallen people who live in a fallen world with other fallen creatures. We have all been wounded. And we all have the capacity to wound others. With each wound that we receive (or give), our pile of emotional garbage grows a little or a lot, depending on the nature of the wound.

The acceptance of this truth is the first step toward healing. It's also the most difficult one for most of us to come to terms with. It's much easier to convince ourselves that we're exempt from the Pile Principle—that we haven't been wounded, or that our wounds haven't left garbage.

As the old saying goes, "Denial is more than just a river in Egypt." It comes in all shapes and sizes, but denial always has one thing in common: we must overcome it. We must see the reality of our woundedness in order to get through the woundedness and gain victory over it. If we don't, we will stay stuck where we are.

In order to better face the reality of our woundedness, let's take a closer look at the three sources of emotional wounds I mentioned briefly in chapter 3.

*Things said to us*

"Sticks and stones may break my bones but words will never hurt me," might sound good on the playground, but we all know it isn't true. If it were true, most of us would be in much better shape. Few of us have received any lasting wounds from sticks and stones, but most—if not all—of us have seen wounded by words. The impact of words in our lives can be seen from the earliest days on the playground when other children hurled hurtful epitaphs at us, such as "fatty," "ugly," "stupid," and the like. Or perhaps a teacher spoke negatively about our ability to learn, and that created a wound. The tongue's negative impact is often demonstrated in hurtful and degrading things that parents say to children. These words become recordings that we unconsciously play back all the way into adulthood. They can direct our lives and destroy our lives if they are never confronted and countered with truth.

For instance, for most of my life I have had a recording that clicks on at times entitled, "Poor white trash." I grew up believing that's all I was, and then this belief was reinforced by the words and attitudes of others. Most of the things I have accomplished in my life have been done within the context of a struggle to drown out its screech. This recording has been a relentless force for most of my life in defining how I see myself. Even now, if I am not careful it will begin to play.

A close friend from college and seminary days is an example of the other end of the social spectrum. Unlike me, he was always "the good kid." He always got high grades and kept his nose clean; he was a leader in his church youth group and was a kid other parents encouraged their kids to emulate. His father was a successful and wealthy businessman, and my friend felt the expectation—and pressure—of reaching a similar level of success with his career. After high school, he went on to college to study for the ministry. After college, he received two graduate degrees from seminary. Today he is a pastor.

While we were in seminary, he began suffering from depression and admitted to having difficulty in relationships. He began to seek help for the emotional wounds he had received from the tongue of his perfectionist, controlling father. During that time, one day between seminary classes he said to me, "James, do you know what my dad did to me one time? When I was sixteen years old he waited until I was completely naked, sitting in the bathtub, and he walked in and said to me, 'Son, you don't really like me and I don't really like you. But until you leave home, here's how it's going to be.'" Then my friend's father proceeded to chart a course for his son's life, laying down a variety of rules and plans the son was expected to keep, follow, and uphold. How's that for creating recordings in your head?

The Bible has a great deal to say about the tongue and its power. One example is James 3, where the tongue is compared with a rudder on a ship, a bit in a horse's mouth, and a small spark that can set a forest on fire. The tongue might be small, but its power is unmatched. The things that people say to us can create deep emotional wounds that direct our lives if they are not addressed.

The question to ask ourselves and others is: "Have we admitted how we've been hurt by what's been said to and about us?"

*Things done to us*

Those of us in counseling circles know that often, although not always, wounded people become wounders. A cycle of abuse and cruelty can continue unchecked generation after generation. The deepest wounds are often perpetrated upon the most vulnerable in our world, the children. Each year, there are hundreds of thousands of reported cases of sexual, physical, and emotional abuse against children in our society.[1] Many other cases go unreported. The majority of men and women at the Hospital Church who reveal that they were sexually or physically abused as a child never told anyone about it before coming to our church.

Some statistics report that more than one-third of all males and as many as one-half of all females will experience some form of sexual abuse by the time they are eighteen years of age.[2] In light of this, it's not unlikely that the average pastor on any given Sunday will be speaking to a crowd where the *majority* have suffered the emotional damage of sexual, physical, or emotional abuse in their past. Most have never told anyone about it, much less gotten any help. Why haven't they? Because they never felt

---

1. See, e.g., U.S. Department of Health and Human Services, "Summary, Child Maltreatment, 2006," at http://www.acf.hhs.gov/programs/cb/pubs/cm06/summary.htm.
2. See, e.g., Advocates for Youth, "Child Sexual Abuse I: An Overview," comp. by Susan K. Finn, January 1995, at http://www.advocatesforyouth.org/PUBLICATIONS/factsheet/fsabuse1.htm.

that it was safe to speak about it and deal with its aftermath in their lives.

*Things taken from us*

The losses of life can also be wounding experiences that cause us damage. Losses can take many forms, such as the loss of a career, of a loved one through divorce or death, or of a reputation through slander and gossip. In some cases it can be the loss of childhood, when the child had to grow up far too early in life.

The bottom line is that everyone has a pile of garbage. It may be a small pile. It may be a huge pile. One thing is for sure: nobody walks through this world without taking some hits. Those hits create wounds that require specific, strategic healing.

If the emotional-spiritual principle is true, then churches are completely overlooking a vital part of ministry to the total person if we are not providing appropriate ministry for the healing of those wounds. So many of the problems that are evident in the marriages and homes of Christians are directly related to these kinds of issues that have never been addressed. Week after week people sit in our churches, covering up the pain of their wounds with a smile and a wave, because the church is not a safe place for them to deal with their wounds.

That doesn't need to be the case.

### Truth #2: Over time, our piles of garbage begin to rot and stink.

Garbage stinks! This only makes sense because garbage is made up of the refuse of life. In your garbage at home you deposit banana peels, the ends of the tomato that you sliced off, and the leftovers from meals that you couldn't put down the disposal. If you remove it quickly, it doesn't have a chance to stink up the house. But if it sits there day after day, it begins to smell—and smell bad.

The pile of emotional garbage that we each carry through life is also made up of the refuse of life. It's the leftovers of painful experiences and memories; the banana peels, tomato trimmings, and leftovers from the things people have said to us or about us, done to us, and taken from us. As this garbage collects, it also begins to rot and stink. As it rots, it creates an unpleasant environment that affects every aspect of our lives. It needs to be set out by the curb so the collectors can take it where it belongs, the garbage dump.

The tragedy is, while few of us would let a pile of stinking garbage smell up our house for very long, we are often willing to carry our stinking, decaying pile of emotional garbage through our entire lives. Perhaps we don't do so willingly but have decided that we just don't have any other choice.

Yet, there is an option. We can take the garbage out!

***Truth #3: When you interact with others, your pile interacts with their pile.***

There is a very valid reason for this truth. My pile goes everywhere I go, and its stench stays with me twenty-four hours a day. The same is true for you. The effects may be minor, or they may be severe, depending upon the amount of garbage and the nature of the relationship. Usually, the more intimate the relationship, the more impact each person's pile has on that relationship and on each other. The deepest impacts are typically seen in the most intimate of all human relationships, marriage.

When two people join themselves in marriage, they also join their individual piles of emotional garbage. If they bring particularly sizeable piles into the relationship, the impact begins to be seen very early on and tends to be deeply hurtful. These two people then begin to wound each other in the relationship and that just adds to their collective pile. Over time, as this emotional garbage pile continues to grow, it continues to rot and stink until eventually it is so massive that it permeates and defines the entire relationship.

This is compounded by the fact that we, often unknowingly, are drawn to people whose particular pile of emotional garbage is especially destructive to us. It is a pathological pull, where my particular pathology draws me like a magnet to someone who has a pathology that is going to be particularly harmful to me. Another way of saying it is, "A deep unmet need in me seeks out a deep unmet need in you." When we get together, all we have done is compounded the unmet need in both of us. Nothing is made better. Everything is compounded.

For instance, Person A who has a strong need for approval will often end up with Person B who is emotionally distant and unable, or unwilling, to give healthy approval and affirmation. Person A longs for approval, seeks for approval, pushes for approval, especially from those reticent to give it. Person B moves away or expresses disapproval, especially toward those who are desperate for approval—the exact opposite of what Person A wanted.

Sometimes, a woman who has been abused in one relationship will move into relationship after relationship with other abusive men. This pattern makes no sense to anyone, including her. She hates the abuse, but like a moth to the flame she continues to be drawn to men who abuse. The need in her may be a need to be connected to a man at any cost (co-dependency), and since she doesn't feel worthy of honor and respect (poor self-esteem), she keeps ending up with men who don't respect and honor women. This fits her pathology and at the same time confirms it for her! These things are not conscious but are so deeply ingrained in her that they continue to happen. Of course, these men abuse because of the emotional garbage they have collected in their lives. They are often passing on the abuse that they have received. The wounded becomes the one who wounds. It's a clear expression of the pathological pull. I have seen this cycle demonstrated in the lives of hundreds of people over the last thirty years of pastoral ministry.

***Truth #4: After a while, we don't smell our own garbage anymore.***

This is where the problem of denial really begins to kick in. If you live with a smell long enough, you become desensitized to it and stop smelling it. The technical term for this is "olfactory desensitization." Perhaps you have seen how this works.

I grew up in West Texas, where the smell of oil can sometimes be overpowering. People who were not from around there would comment about it, but I had breathed it for so long I didn't even notice it. To us locals it was just the smell of money.

But I'll never forget the experience of smelling my first paper mill. One of my college roommates was getting married, and there was a paper mill near the small town in Louisiana where the wedding was to be held. My wife and I drove into that little town, and the smell hit us like a ton of bricks. I remember thinking, "How do these people live with this smell?"

Well, the way they live with it is the same way I lived with the oil smell: they don't smell it anymore.

Recently, my wife bought me a little device for my office that is designed to counter olfactory desensitization. I love having fresh scents in my office. I don't care for the musty smell that a closed room takes on. So she bought me a motorized scent distribution device that is ingenious. It uses a cartridge that has four complementary scents in it. Every thirty minutes it rotates the cartridge to another scent. Just about the time my nose becomes desensitized to one scent, it changes to another one. That way, all day long I can smell the fresh and pleasing scents on a rotating basis.

For someone living in the West Texas oil fields or near Louisiana paper mills, it's an act of the grace of God that the scent doesn't rotate every thirty minutes. Nobody could live in either place!

When it comes to our pile of emotional garbage we have a tendency to quickly become desensitized to the stench of what we're carrying around with us. This results in us going through life blaming all our problems on other people. Interestingly enough, even though I might not smell my own garbage anymore, I don't become desensitized to the smell of everyone else's garbage. I smell it just fine!

Jesus indicated this tendency in the Sermon on the Mount when He dealt with the problem of judging. In Matthew 7:3, He asks, "Why do you look at the speck that is in your brother's eye, but do not notice the log that is in your own eye?" The simple answer is, I have lived with this log in my eye for so long that I have developed ways of looking around it. I have lived my life compensating for it for so long that I don't even notice it.

The same holds true with the pile of emotional garbage we carry. Here, for instance, is how it often works itself out in a marriage context. One partner looks at the other and says, "If you would just deal with your garbage, our marriage would be better!" Then they fill in the blank: "If you didn't——. If you weren't——. If you would just——." On and on it goes. At the same time the other partner is saying the same thing in the other direction. Neither of the partners recognizes his or her own garbage because each has lived with it so long it's not smelled anymore. Accusations fly, fingers get pointed, relationships deteriorate, and a marriage that was entered into with the intention that it would be *Little House on the Prairie* becomes *Nightmare on Elm Street*.

### Truth #5: Each one of us has to deal with our own pile of emotional garbage,

More than twenty years ago, the odyssey of a barge called the Mobro 4000 dominated the attention of our entire nation. On March 22, 1987, the Mobro set out on a 6,000-mile voyage to find a place to dump 3,200 tons of garbage that nobody wanted. Do the math—that's a boatload of 6.4 million pounds of stinking garbage!

The trouble all began when the garbage dump in the city of Islip, New York, got full. So the pile was loaded on the Mobro and the ship set out looking for a new home for their garbage. At first it was thought that Morehead City, North Carolina, might take the garbage and turn it into methane fuel. That proved to be a smelly rumor. The Mobro then set off for Louisiana, but Louisiana wanted none of it. Then it was down to Mexico, where the Mexican navy met the garbage barge in the Yucatan Channel, forbidding it to even enter Mexican waters. Belize also refused to let the Mobro dock. Off to the Bahamas, but the Bahamas wouldn't have it. Before it was over, the Mobro had been rejected by six states and three countries and had to turn around and go back to New York.

On May 16, after two months at sea, the trash arrived back in New York. But its troubles were still not over. The New Yorkers weren't excited about seeing their garbage show back up on their doorstep. (By this time things were really ripe.) The Mobro wanted to dock near Queens, where the plan was that trucks could carry it back to where it came from in Islip, but the president of the Borough of Queens said not a chance! She didn't even want the garbage to pass through Queens. She obtained a restraining order preventing the barge from even docking. Eventually, in July, the federal government granted the Mobro a federal anchorage in New Jersey. Finally, when all the court challenges had ended, the Mobro made its way back up to Brooklyn, New York, where the garbage was incinerated. On September 1, the first truckload of ash was deposited on the landfill in Islip where five months earlier it had been launched out to sea in hopes that it might become someone else's problem.

And that's the moral of the Mobro. In the end, Islip had to deal with its own garbage. At the heart of the Pile Principle is the core value that each of us must, in the end, deal with our own garbage. No one can do it for us.

Here's a ridiculous question: How much sense would it make if I went up and down my block, knocking on doors, asking, "Can I take out your garbage?" while my own garbage was collecting and piling up outside my garage. My neighbors might eventually catch on and say something like, "Hey, buddy, why don't you worry about your own garbage and let me take care of mine?" That would be a good question, because at the end of the day the only garbage that each of us is really responsible for is our own.

In recovery circles we refer to this as "keeping your own side of the street clean." Don't always be trying to clean up the other guy's side. Just take care of your own. That's all you are able to do anything about anyway.

Since marriage is the relationship where emotional garbage does its greatest damage, I'll use the illustration of marriage to explain how keeping your own side of the street clean works.

There are certain issues that every marriage must negotiate. They are the big ones that are usually said to be the top three causes of marital discord and divorce: sex, money, and in-laws. But both spouses have to be at some minimum level of emotional health[3] before they can even begin to negotiate these normal issues of marriage.

What often happens is this: When a couple gets to the point of desperation about one or all three of these issues (or it may be about some other issue), they will go to a marriage counselor. This is sometimes the worst thing they can do. I don't mean that good Christian counseling isn't valuable. It certainly is. I mean that this couple may not be healthy enough individually to get any value out of the marriage counseling! Especially if the counseling focuses only on the marriage issues. Those issues are not the primary issues. They are the presenting problems of the deeper issues related to their individual piles of emotional garbage that they each brought to the relationship. Often a good and wise counselor will recognize this and recommend seeing the spouses separately for a time before they continue counseling as a couple. If the counselor does not recognize this, the couple may go for a few sessions, see no progress, and give up. The end result isn't good.

What needs to happen is that each individual begins to smell his or her own garbage. Then each individual can begin the work of reducing his or her own pile. This process includes freedom group work (which will be discussed in depth in chapter 7), and sometimes also good Christian counseling, usually group counseling. My experience is that involvement in a good freedom group with fellow strugglers, where people use biblically based, thought-provoking material under the guidance of a good facilitator, can bring some of the greatest healing of all. When each spouse has reduced his or her individual piles to a reasonable level, then they can come together and begin to address the issues that have been created in the marriage.

---

3. This "minimum level" is not objectively quantifiable; it is individual but becomes obvious in relationships.

Over the years, I have seen the approach of two individuals in a marriage focusing on their own emotional garbage separately become a successful strategy for saving a marriage. The first time I saw it happen was almost three decades ago. One of the guys who had been instrumental in leading me to Christ had been my freshman college roommate. Then we both transferred to Baylor University at the same time. We were in seminary together. I was in his wedding, and he was in my wedding. He married a girl from our hometown, and everything seemed to be going well. One day, while we were still in seminary, he called me and asked me to come over to their apartment. He informed me that his wife wanted a separation. I was devastated. So was he.

She had told him that they had individual issues that needed to be dealt with and marriage issues that needed to be addressed. She wanted to separate while they were in the midst of that process. They did separate, and it lasted about six months. During that time they each reached into the garbage pile and began to deal with their own stuff. Doing that eventually allowed them to deal with the marriage garbage they had created together. Today, they have eight children and are as happily married as any couple I know.

## HOPE AHEAD

Over the past number of years in the Hospital Church, I have explained the pile principle to couples many times and seen its ability to save relationships demonstrated. One of the most attractive, talented, and outwardly successful-looking couples in my church have walked through this process with success. Their situation was the classic pattern at work—on the outside, everything in their life initially looked shipshape. Matt and Emily were in their upper twenties with two young children and were actively involved in leadership in our ministry to other young couples. We even sent other couples to them for counsel. But there were problems in paradise that nobody knew about. Emotional wounds and garbage were wreaking havoc. The piles had built up and had not been dealt with.

Emily was raised in a Christian home and professed Christ years before she met Matt. She had been severely hurt as a young girl and had made some bad choices along the way before she and Matt were married. Matt had come to know Christ later in life. All through his growing up years, his parents were heavy party people. Drinking and drugs had been a part of his environment since he had been a young boy. He followed in their footsteps through teen years and into young adulthood. Matt and Emily's piles of refuse began to stink, and their marriage felt the strain. For a time, they separated.

Emily began the freedom group process to deal with her emotional pain. She also began to see a caring and compassionate female Christian counselor. As she dealt with her pile of emotional garbage and experienced emotional healing, she began to see the truth about her "happy Christian marriage." In truth, it was a sham. It looked good to everyone on the outside, but it was diseased from the inside. She loved her husband, but as a result of the unresolved emotional issues of his past, he was obsessive-compulsive in his relationship to her and acted out in destructive ways, including being controlling and verbally and emotionally abusive. She recognized that her own pathology had led her to a co-dependent relationship with her husband that was more like parent-child than husband-wife. She was getting healthy enough to see the truth now.

Matt couldn't smell his pile of garbage. In his mind, it was all about Emily. She had all the problems. In a counseling session with him, I took off the gloves and told this young man that if he didn't come out of denial to recognize and deal with his issues, his marriage was over. He got angry at me, and his parents went back and forth about how they felt toward me. One day his father would agree that his son needed help. The next day he would be angry with me for what I was doing in "completely taking her side." But I wasn't taking her side. I was taking the side of the marriage.

Over time, mostly out of desperation, Matt began the process and went to that same counselor. I encouraged him also to become a part of a men's freedom group that was just beginning at our church. The group was designed to help the members experience emotional healing of hurtful past experiences. He agreed. Over the next thirteen weeks, the truth began to come out, the wall of denial began to come down, and the stench of his own garbage began to reach his nose.

With that, the healing began in earnest. The work was by no means finished for them individually or as a couple. But now they could do the work. They had become intimately aware of their own respective pile of garbage and had begun to work on their individual piles. That opened the way for them to deal with the garbage that had been created in the marriage. They are now on their way to building a lasting, healthy marriage.

A hospital church ministry is a place where this kind of healing can take place openly, without judgment. Even for a couple like Matt and Emily, who were seen as leaders. Now their leadership will be able to be real leadership, not leadership based on a lie, but hammered out with transparency and truth.

People are shocked when I tell them that on any given Sunday there are any number of couples in our church who are separated but are both in church at the same time. They don't live together, they don't drive to church together, and they often don't even sit together in church. But they are received, accepted, loved, and supported in what they are doing to save their marriage. They don't slink in embarrassed. They don't sit on the back row. They don't wear a scarlet letter. Church has become a safe place to do the necessary work of individual healing and healing in their marriage. It's really incredible when I stop to think about it. That's the kind of safe place created by embracing the core values of hospital church style ministry: a place where people who are really trying to grow and change are embraced and valued.

The work in any hospital church ministry is based upon the recognition of the emotional-spiritual principle and the Pile Principle. The emotional-spiritual connection recognizes the impact that our emotional wounds have on our spiritual relationship to God. The Pile Principle recognizes the impact that our emotional wounds (or emotional garbage piles) have on our human relationships. When we recognize both and begin to deal with the wounds, the way is opened for both kinds of relationships to blossom into all that the Father desires them to be.

That is the calling and the passion of the Hospital Church.

# PART FOUR

# The Basics

CHAPTER 6

# How Change Happens

I recently attended summer camp with the youth group from our church. The camp wasn't exactly what we hoped it was going to be. The teachers there said some things during the week that really stretched us all. It required that I spend some time at night giving balance to what the kids were hearing.

One night the teacher spoke about some things that are issues in virtually every group of teenagers (or adults, for that matter) in our day. He spoke of the pain of abandonment, from parents who had gone away or parents who had stayed physically but had never been present emotionally. He said some students had done things in their past that they still carried shame and guilt over, even though they had confessed them to God. Some struggled with the inner pain of abuse. Many used language that was not honoring to them, to others, or to God. He did an excellent job of covering all kinds of problems that kids in that room certainly would be dealing with. Then he invited any of the students who identified with what he had just said and wanted to be set free, to stand so that people could pray for them. I was beginning to feel a little concern, because I feared where he was heading, but I still felt that it would be great for kids to be able to stand in a group like that and receive prayer and support from their peers, as well as from the adults who were present.

All over the room, students began to stand. Some were in tears. One young man a couple of rows in front of me stood for prayer because his father had left him and his mother when he was a young boy. That abandonment had created a hole in his heart that still affected him. He was so emotionally moved that his shoulders were shaking with his sobs. I could relate with his pain because I too had felt the abandonment of an alcoholic father. When the leader called for people to gather around that young man and pray for him, I didn't even hesitate. Five or six of us gathered around him and began to pray. I prayed for his broken heart and anger and asked the heavenly Father to surround him right then with His love. I was moved to be able to pray for him, he was moved, and I believe the heart of the Father was moved in that moment.

But then things headed south quickly. The teacher declared to the young man that from that moment on he would be completely set free from his shame, anger, and unforgiveness toward his father for abandoning him and his mother. It was given as a declaration of fact, that from that moment on he was done. Then, for the next thirty minutes around the room, each student who was standing was prayed for by people around them and then declared by the teacher to be released.

What concerned me about this were the implications of such a declaration. If everyone who had been prayed for was instantly healed and released, then there would never need to be any more work done. There would never be any more healing that would need to take place. They would walk out of that room with no emotional wounds or devastation in the future. That concerned me because that is not what I believe about the normal process of how change happens. Were these kids being set up for a fall? I believe so.

## WELCOME TO PLAN B

That night, as our kids gathered in our group, it was obvious that some of our kids were upset. I was upset too. We discussed how real change happens. Is it an event or a process? Certainly God is able to instantly deliver someone from shame, unforgiveness, guilt, or a propensity to use vulgar speech. Scripture certainly records instances of Jesus healing the physical wounds of people instantaneously. He could do that with any kind of healing, physical or emotional. The question here isn't His ability. It is about how he normally chooses to work in the area of life change today.

There is something in us that wants change to be an instantaneous event, rather than a process in which we must participate. It would be easier, quicker, and, from the human perspective, more desirable, if change was always an event. But, frankly, that's not how God most often chooses to work. That night at camp provided an opportunity for me to teach our students some of the basic truths that will be discussed in this chapter. This is the model of change we operate from in the Hospital Church.

When I first read Henry Cloud and John Townsend's excellent work *How People Grow* I was encouraged by what they had to say on the subject of change.[1] In the early pages, Cloud gives his testimony about his struggle with change. He mentions that for many years after he became a Christian he prayed for God to remove his depression and just make him feel better. He says that he had this idea that God had a plan A and a plan B for healing hurts. If you were special to God, you got God's plan A. He would instantaneously zap you and take away what was hurting you in your life. Obviously, the teacher at our camp subscribed to "plan A" theology.

Cloud prayed and prayed and prayed for plan A. It didn't happen. So what about if you don't get God's plan A? Then you have to settle for plan B. Plan B says that change happens over the course of time and through the instrumentality of other people. Cloud didn't want any of plan B. He wanted God's

---

1. Henry Cloud and John Townsend, *How People Grow: What the Bible Reveals about Personal Growth* (Grand Rapids: Zondervan, 2001). We use this book in one of our support groups in the Hospital Church.

plan A. He wanted an event, not a process. It didn't happen for him that way, and it doesn't seem to happen that way for very many of us.

Cloud then tells how he came in contact with some people who began to gather around him in his life. They began to invest in him, teach him, share with him, love him, and allow him to be honest and transparent about his life and his hurts. In time, Cloud realized that the emptiness he had been feeling was really sadness and hurt. As he got in touch with those hurts and that emptiness, he began to deal with forgiveness issues. As he walked through that process, great burdens began to be lifted off his shoulders. During this time he also got connected with a small group where he could continue his honesty and where they would be honest with him.

So for Cloud the pattern of healing was:

*Pain* led him to seek *help*.

*Help* was found within *community*.

The *community* provided trust and support, which enabled him to be *honest* about what was really happening.

The more *honest* he was, the more in touch with God's *truth* he was.

Being in touch with God's *truth* allowed him to begin to *admit* he had been hurt and was empty, which allowed him to begin to *forgive* the people who had hurt him.

When he *forgave*, the burdens lifted.

His true emotional healing began.

Eventually he realized his depression and feelings of emptiness were becoming less and less severe. In time, they were virtually gone. He said, "I was both happy and disappointed with that realization"[2] God had changed his life and for that he was happy, but he was disappointed when he realized he had gotten God's plan B healing!

Then he began to study the Scripture about this issue and discovered that what he had considered plan B was God's plan A all along! Most often God chooses to work over the course of time and through people. This doesn't mean that people bring the healing. It doesn't deny the supernatural source of true change and healing. In fact, it embraces that source in all His fullness and in recognition that this is His sovereign will. God chooses most often to do His work through people as His instruments.

Cloud's story reminds me of a statement that was reportedly written on the wall of a twelve-step meeting hall. It read, "Welcome to plan B. If plan A had worked, none of us would be here!" Plan A refers to all the attempts at white-knuckling sobriety in people's own power and strength. So welcome to plan B. Thank God for plan B.

When you understand the connection we explored in the emotional-spiritual discussion (chapter 4), then it only makes sense that God would choose to do most of His healing work through other people. By using people as instruments of healing in our lives, God furthers and deepens our connection with each other as we become instruments of His healing to each other. Perhaps that is what Paul meant when he said in Ephesians 4:15–16, "But speaking the truth in love we are to grow up in all aspects into Him, who is the head, even Christ, from whom the whole body, being fitted and held together by what every joint supplies, according to the proper working of each individual part, causes the growth of the body for the building up of itself in love."

## THE SAME THING OVER AND OVER

A basic truth of human nature is that we typically fight and resist change with nearly everything that is within us, even when the change is good! We may hate our life as it is, but we

---

2. Cloud and Townsend, *How People Grow,* 119.

will continue to do the same things that have gotten us into our sorry state because at least the misery we are in is familiar. What life would be like if change happened is unknown, unfamiliar—and it is this that frightens us most of all.

Because of this fear, it usually takes a powerful motivating force to move us to change. That force often is pain. As much as we hate change, we hate pain even more, especially intense pain. We will do nearly anything to avoid it. When we can't avoid it, we will deny it or temporarily medicate it with some addiction, compulsive behavior, or chemical. The truth is that we don't respond to information, we respond to pain. We can be told that there is a better way to do life, but that is just information. Information doesn't motivate to change. It is only when the pain of the life that we are currently living becomes so great that we are no longer willing to bear it that we are usually willing to change.

Sometimes, someone will come into my office to tell me the story of their life. Every pastor experiences it. The stories may include failed marriages, estrangement from children, loss of career or business, financial struggle, guilt, remorse, sadness, and various addictions. At the end of the story I'll always ask the question, "Well, how's it working out for you?"

They'll say, "How's what working out for me?"

"How are the things that you are doing working out for you? Do you like the results you are getting?"

The answer is almost always no. My response, "Then change what you're doing."

Albert Einstein is often attributed as saying that the definition of insanity is doing the same thing over and over thinking you are going to get a different result. By that definition most of us suffer from some level of insanity.

Something has to happen that will cause us to look at the results we are getting from the things we are doing and ask ourselves the question, "How's it working out for me?" It's not only pain but intense pain that is usually necessary before we come to that level of honesty. A friend of mine referred to it as "the scorched earth syndrome" in his life. Why does it so often take a scorched earth to get us to change?

Recently, I heard pastor and author Wayne Cordeiro honestly and openly speak about his own experience of pain. He had worked himself to near breakdown. He burned the candle at both ends as a high-capacity, high-achieving person. It brought him to near physical and emotional meltdown. That led him to a reorientation of his life in virtually every area. He said, "Sometimes the only way radical change happens is through radical pain." That has been my observation in my own life and in the lives of hundreds of others through the years.

## YOU TELL 'EM I'M COMIN'

The Old Testament story of Jacob illustrates this scorched-earth syndrome. Jacob means "deceiver or schemer." If anyone has ever lived down to his name, it was Jacob. Most of his life was spent in lying, scheming, and manipulating to get what he wanted. In the end, the consequences of that life caught up with him, and that is when change began to happen.

Jacob's scheming days began when he deceived his father, Isaac, and stole the blessing from his older brother, Esau (Gen. 27). It's a scenario worthy of Broadway, complete with the use of props, sets, and drama, and it caused an immediate relationship failure with Esau. Because of that deception, Esau hated his brother and spent a great deal of his own life trying to rid the earth of his brother's presence.

Then Jacob found himself on the receiving end of the deception when he came up against another schemer named Laban (Gen. 29:21–35). Jacob desired to marry Laban's daughter, Rachel, and agreed to serve Laban for seven years in return for her hand. But when all was said and done, Laban had not only gotten an extra seven years of service out of Jacob, but he had also pawned off his other, harder-to-marry daughter, Leah. The schemer had been schemed.

Jacob wasn't about to be outdone. Later, he devised a plan by which he could cheat his father-in-law out of the best of the flocks and herds (Gen. 30:25–43). When Laban discovered what had happened, Jacob had to hotfoot it out of town. This was the second time his deceiving ways had caused him to put the city limits in his rearview mirror. How's it working out for Jacob? Not really very well, except that he has accumulated a lot of stuff by this time. All of that wealth was going to be cold comfort for him before this saga ended.

Soon, it all unraveled. Jacob had lied, deceived, and schemed himself into a corner. Esau had been relentless in his pursuit of revenge for Jacob's deception. Jacob had run about as far as he could run. So he decided to make a last-ditch attempt at buying Esau off. He gathered an enormous number from his flocks and herds and sent them out as a peace offering to Esau. Even with that, Jacob seems to have known intuitively that it wasn't going to pacify Esau, because then he sent his wives and children away for their own safety.

In Genesis 32:24, we read these seemingly innocuous but ominous words, "Then Jacob was left alone." Jacob was faced with the inevitable result of his life of deception. He was wealthy for sure, but he was also alone—hated by his brother, only tolerated by his father-in-law, and now he had to send his own family away to protect them from the harmful results of his deception. The consequences were mounting up. That people eventually go away is always the consequence of all destructive behavior. Bridges get burned, and just like Jacob we become isolated—if not physically, at least emotionally.

Jacob was in real danger of losing his life. Esau didn't even wink an eye at Jacob's attempt to buy him off. Esau came with a fury and had four hundred men with him. His anger had plenty of time to burn, and he wanted blood. When I think of Esau's anger, I'm reminded of the statement Kurt Russell made in the Hollywood movie *Tombstone*. Wyatt Earp, the character Russell played, had his fill of the outlaw gang called the Cowboys. He stands and announces, "You tell 'em I'm comin'. You tell 'em I'm comin' and Hell's comin' with me."[3] That probably summed up Esau's attitude toward Jacob.

---

3. *Tombstone*, directed by George P. Cosmatos (Santa Monica, CA: Cinergi Pictures Entertainment, 1993).

Imagine what this must have been like for Jacob. He's sitting by the campfire all night by himself, thinking. He probably doesn't care much for time alone. Nobody else likes Jacob, and he probably doesn't care much for himself either. I can imagine a thought something like this going through his mind, "Man, this is getting old. I am so tired of being on the run. I am tired of the conflict. I am just tired!" He is facing the consequences of his actions, and for the first time he can't lie or scheme his way out. How's it working out for you? Congratulations, Jacob. What a great place to be.

*I know what some of you are thinking: "Congratulations!? Is this guy crazy?"* Nop I'm not. This was the best place Jacob could possibly be. It is only when a person comes to the end of himself that he can come to the beginning of God, and the beginning of real change. Jesus said in Matthew 5:3, "Blessed are the poor in spirit, for theirs is the kingdom of heaven." The word for "poor" that Jesus uses means "destitute" in the original language. Blessed are the destitute of spirit. It isn't the poverty of someone who has a little. It is the poverty of total and complete emptiness and destitution! Christ means, "When you are willing to come to me empty-handed, admitting that you have nothing to offer me, that you are destitute, at the end of yourself, then you are blessed! When you are emptied of yourself, then you can be filled with all I have to offer."

There is a blessedness in brokenness. It's difficult for us to wrap our minds around that concept, but it is nevertheless true. However, Jacob hadn't reached brokenness yet. He was on the path but hasn't yet reached the destination. Sometimes we confuse the process with the end result.

## CLOSE, BUT NOT QUITE THERE YET

Several years ago I became acquainted with a successful and popular man. He was in demand as a teacher, public speaker, and facilitator of groups. It seemed he was on top of the world. But there was a crack in the foundation. That crack became a fissure, and the foundation broke when he crossed a moral boundary. His house came crashing down around his ears. There were some inner issues that had never been resolved, which had made him a ticking time bomb for this kind of failure. It hadn't been a matter of if this would happen but when.

And it happened. When the dust had settled, someone recommended that he come and speak with me about putting the pieces of his life back together at the Hospital Church. Our meeting didn't go quite the way he planned. Early into our conversation it became obvious to me that he was still angry and pointing the finger of blame at everyone but the one person who was really culpable, himself. He had his anger focused at God, the church, and, if it would have helped, the mailman who delivered his mail!

I said to him, "I don't think there is much that can be done to help you right now because you have not yet come to brokenness." That drew an energetic response.

"What are you talking about?! I've lost everything! I've lost my family, my ministry, my job. Everything."

"What you have just described to me is not the experience of brokenness," I said, "but the process. You may be on the way, but you haven't gotten there yet. You are still trying to blame others for your failure. You haven't come to the end of yourself. When you do, we'll be here to help you in any way we can." (This is the Pile Principle in action. A person must own his own pile.)

To my knowledge, this man is still fighting the blessing of brokenness. His response to the pain is still anger and blaming others for what has happened in his life. The pain still hasn't become intense enough to motivate him toward real change. Some people have a higher tolerance for pain than others.

Now back to Jacob. He was isolated and facing an impossible situation, but he hadn't come to the point of brokenness yet. He was well on his the way, but just not there yet. God knew he was ripe for the picking, so in the night He waylaid Jacob. As he was sitting by the campfire, with no company but his own, and probably not enjoying that very much, God pounced on him. Genesis 32:24 describes a man wrestling with Jacob all night long. (We read in Hosea 12:3–4 that the man is an angel of the Lord.)

Jacob had been fighting his whole life, and he wasn't going to go down easily, even if his opponent was God. They wrestled all night and into the morning. Eventually the angel touched the socket of Jacob's thigh and dislocated it (Gen. 32:25). Without his legs, Jacob was done. An army moves on its feet, and a wrestler must have his legs. Jacob couldn't fight anymore. All he could do was cling to the angel and announce that he wouldn't let go until the angel blessed him (v. 26).

It has always intrigued me that this match went on all night long. The angel could have ended this thing in the first round. He could have dislocated Jacob's thigh in the first moment of the bout rather than after it had lasted for hours.

I believe the fight lasted all night for Jacob's sake. Up until the dislocation, Jacob was still holding out hope that he might win. But this was a fight Jacob couldn't afford to win. So the angel let it carry on and carry on. Then, in one touch, he subdued Jacob and broke him. End of match! Ring the bell. Throw in the towel. Jacob is toast.

The angel asked, "What is your name?" (v. 27). That was an interesting question at this time in the story, for surely the angel knew with whom he had been tussling all night. The question wasn't for the angel's information; it was a reminder for Jacob of who he was. Jacob replied, "Jacob." Remember that means "schemer, liar, deceiver, heel grabber." It's as if the Lord was saying, "That's right. That's who you are and who you have been all of your life. Admit it. Own it. How's it working out for you?"

The angel replied, "Your name shall no longer be called Jacob but Israel; for you have struggled with God and with men, and have prevailed" (v. 28). Israel means "Prince with God." Jacob went from "deceiver" to "prince with God." He lost the fight, but he won the war. He lost the wrestling match, but in his brokenness he was the winner. He experienced the blessing of brokenness. That was God's purpose all along for Jacob. For most of his life, Jacob had fought that purpose—just as so many of us do.

## THE GOOD THAT PAIN CAN BRING

While I believe this event with Jacob wrestling the angel really happened, I also see it as a metaphor of our struggle against coming to the end of ourselves. We fight the pain and the consequences of our actions, and we stiffen our necks against giving up until God allows our hip to be dislocated and we are broken. We fight with God, but it is a fight that none of us can afford to win. The irony is that only when we give up the fight do we win the war. We win everything good that God desires us to have. Hebrews 11:21 says that when Jacob blessed his sons at the end of his life he "worshiped, leaning on the top of his staff." I love that. It indicates that Jacob walked with a limp for the rest of his life. God gave him a reminder of his brokenness. Perhaps, like Paul's thorn in the flesh, Jacob's limp served to remind him of his need to be weak.

In the Hospital Church, we have come to recognize and even celebrate the value of pain. Pain is a good thing because pain tells us that something is wrong. Pain is like the oil light in your car. When it flashes on, either you need to put oil in the crankcase, or you need a new oil pump. Whichever it is, you can't afford to ignore the light, or you will destroy your engine.

Pain is God's oil light. As C. S. Lewis wrote in *The Problem of Pain*, "God whispers to us in our pleasures, speaks to us in our conscience, but shouts in our pains. It is his megaphone to rouse a deaf world."[4] Pain is the shout of God saying, "Something is wrong" and asking, "How's it working out for you?"

If you don't like the results you are getting, then change what you are doing.

## BETWEEN THE EARS

Before change can happen in our lives, change must first happen in our minds. Actions don't just spring up out of nowhere. Every action is preceded by a thought. The way we live and act is determined by how we think, and the way we think is most often guided by the experiences we have had in life. Trying to change your actions and behaviors without changing your patterns of thinking is like trying to kill a weed by chopping the top off. The weed disappears for a short while and then springs back. You have to dig a weed out by its roots. In the same way, anyone

---

4. C. S. Lewis, *The Problem of Pain* (New York: Harper Collins, 2001), 91.

can strong-arm a change in behavior for a short period of time. But without a change in thinking, that change will almost always be temporary. The root of destructive and unhealthy behaviors is destructive thinking. It's what Zig Zigler, the popular motivational speaker, used to call "stinkin' thinkin'."

Stinkin' thinkin' results in stinkin' livin'. To explain this truth, and how it affects the work that goes on in a hospital church ministry, I want to point to two key passages of Scripture that have informed me and challenged me throughout my ministry. The first is Romans 12:1–2, and the second is 2 Corinthians 10:3–5. These two passages, and others along the way, express the vital importance of the mind in seeing how real change happens. At the core of what the Hospital Church does is a commitment to help people learn a new way of thinking so they can enter into a new way of living. But this change isn't easy. Real change requires several things from us:

### Change requires an all-out commitment to change

Romans 12:1–2 says, "Therefore I urge you, brethren, by the mercies of God, to present your bodies a living and holy sacrifice, acceptable to God, which is your spiritual service of worship. And do not be conformed to this world, but be transformed by the renewing of your mind, so that you may prove what the will of God is, that which is good and acceptable and perfect."

Let's unpack this passage of Scripture.

The first verse says to "present your bodies a living and holy sacrifice."

This language no longer carries the full impact it would have had in that day. We are too far removed from the environment of sacrificial offerings. The imagery used is of a sacrifice in the Jewish temple. Every day animals were laid on the altar and presented to God. When a sacrifice was offered to God, a transference of ownership took place. It was offered to God and the title deed was essentially signed over. As Christians, we understand that animal sacrifices are no longer necessary because Jesus Christ has offered the final and perfect sacrifice on our behalf on the cross (Heb. 9:11–12). There is now no longer any need for sacrifice. How could you possibly improve upon the perfect sacrifice of Christ's perfect life?

So this passage in Romans 12 isn't about offering dead animal sacrifices but about offering ourselves as living sacrifices. The animal sacrifices of the temple did not offer themselves willingly. In fact, I'm sure that there was often a great struggle getting a lamb or a goat to the point of sacrifice. There was a lot of bleating and baaing going on! Hooves were flying, and teeth were bared. Sacrifice could be a noisy and messy business.

In contrast, Paul presents an image of the sacrifice willingly offering himself. Of his own volition the sacrifice crawls up onto the altar and says, "Here I am! I offer myself! Take me, I am yours. I am transferring ownership. The title deed to everything in my life is signed over to you!"

For real and lasting change to take place, there has to be a voluntary giving over of oneself in that way. Change is serious business. There are no weekend warriors in the life-change process. You have to be willing to crawl up on the altar and give yourself over completely to the process of life transformation. Without that kind of commitment, lasting change is not likely to happen. That is why pain is so important in the change process. This kind of commitment to the process is rare without intense pain to motivate it.

Over the years I have had many people come to me in a crisis, and I turned them away. It may shock you to hear that, but I decided a long time ago that my time, and the work the Hospital Church does, is far too precious to waste on weekend warriors looking for a fast and easy change. Let me explain.

Sometimes a wife or husband who is married to an alcoholic (you can substitute just about any other kind of compulsive, destructive behavior here) will come to the breaking point with his or her addicted spouse. They'll threaten to leave if the spouse doesn't do something to change their behavior. So to make peace, the addict will agree to come in and talk to the pastor. It's like being called in to see the principal. The addict puts on his or her best face and performance, saying all the right things, sometimes crying great crocodile tears, and making promises to cut back or to change, blah blah blah.

I don't mean to sound cynical here, but I've seen this a thousand times. And the reality is that the addicted spouse is not willing to do the things I know are necessary for real change to happen. The addict isn't even there for change, but in order to appease a fed-up spouse. It's all part of the addictive behavior to manipulate and lie and keep the game going. I sometimes will look the addict in the face and say something like this: "You know what you need to do? Go out and just get falling down sloppy drunk. I'm talking commode-hanging, chunk-spewing drunk! Just keep doing that. And after your wife has finally booted you out for the last time, your kids can't stand you, everyone is embarrassed by you, you've lost your job or business, and your health has gone into the toilet, then come back and we'll see what we can do."

In essence what I'm saying is, "You aren't ready to crawl up on the altar and become a living sacrifice. Until you are ready to do that, nothing is going to change." I've had people cuss me out, call me un-Christian, and even threaten to beat me up when I have told them this. But I have learned by experience that people who are looking for Band-Aids to put on spewing arteries never truly change. They don't want it badly enough. They haven't come to the blessedness of brokenness.

There is another word in Romans 12:1 that indicates the importance of total commitment. The text says that we are to present ourselves as "living" sacrifices. In other words, this sacrifice is about life, not death. When we crawl up on the altar in total submission to transformation, we don't lose our life as the sacrifices in the temple did. We gain life!

Jesus said in Luke 9:24, "For whoever wishes to save his life will lose it, but whoever loses his life for My sake, he is the one who will save it." Jesus is talking about more than physical martyrdom in this passage. In the previous verse He said, "If anyone wishes to come after Me, he must deny himself, and take up his cross *daily* and follow Me" (emphasis added). Jesus is talking about being a living sacrifice. It is about being yielded over to whatever He wants to do with me, submitted to whatever adjustment and whatever change He desires to bring.

Change requires an all-out commitment to it.

### Change requires that we identify our destructive patterns of thinking

The next statement in Romans 12:2 is "do not be conformed to this world." A more accurate translation is "*stop* being conformed to this world." The idea isn't to keep from doing something that could potentially happen but to stop something that is already happening. The conforming is already happening. We are called to stop the process. We live in this fallen world under constant pressure to be squeezed into its mold. We are being pressured into its worldly and destructive way of thinking about ourselves, others, and God. For change to happen, those destructive patterns must be identified and changed.

The concept of "the world" in the New Testament isn't about the physical world, it is a system of thinking that is against God. It means all that is in opposition to God and His purposes for His creation. In James 1:27, we are told to remain "unstained by the world." In James 4:4, we are told that "a friend of the world makes himself an enemy of God." In 2 Corinthians 4:4, Satan himself is referred to as the "god of this world," or someone who for a limited time has been given latitude in this world. Satan functions as god over a system that is against all of the good that God desires to do in creation. Make no mistake about it, Satan's time is limited. There will be a day when God with a big *G* puts an end to this world system and all that is in it.

Once you understand the character of the Enemy that rules over this world system, then you can begin to understand how he intends to accomplish his purpose. First of all, Jesus tells us in John 10:10, "The thief comes . . . to steal and kill and destroy." But Jesus came so that people "may have life, and have it abundantly." The Enemy's strategy is to kill, steal, and destroy. Jesus' strategy is to give abundant life.

Jesus also informs us that the Enemy, at his core, is a liar. In John 8:44 Jesus says of Satan, "whenever he speaks a lie, he speaks from his own nature, for he is a liar and the father of lies." If his nature is that of a liar, and if he is the father of lies, then it stands to reason that he will do his work of stealing, killing, and destroying by the use of lies. Satan destroys our lives by convincing us to believe lies about ourselves, others, God, and life.

In the original language of the New Testament, the word used for "conformed" in Romans 12:2 is the Greek word from which we get our English word "schematic." A schematic is a plan or a diagram. In other words, God with a big G has a schematic, and god with a little g, the god of this world, also has a schematic. We are to stop being "schematized" by the world. We are to live according to God's schematic of truth not the Enemy's schematic of lies.

In summary, this verse is telling us to stop allowing ourselves to be pressured into the Enemy's schematic or design (the world), which is against God. Since we know his nature and character is that of a liar, then we know that his schematic, his design, is not the truth but a lie. We also know that his goal is not our good but our demise and destruction. So the Bible says, "Stop being conformed to this world!"

Now I want to make the practical application. We are all born into this world system, and we are raised in this world system of which Satan is "god." We are all under constant pressure from this world to live according to the Enemy's lies that are meant to destroy. Everything around us in this world seeks to conform us into believing, and thus living, according to his lies. Emotionally damaging and hurtful experiences in life are one way those lies are planted in our hearts. Over time those lies begin to inform everything about how we think about ourselves, others, and God. This is why a very important step in the process of emotional healing and maturity is to identify what those lies are, what experiences in life planted them in us, and how those lies are currently having negative and damaging effects on our lives.

For life change to happen there must be mind change. This principle is illustrated clearly in the history of Israel in the Old Testament. God delivered the Israelites from Egypt after four hundred years of slavery. After a short time in the wilderness, they came to Kadesh-Barnea just across the Jordan River from the land that He had promised them. Numbers 13–14 records how God instructed them to send twelve spies into the land to scope it out. One leader out of each of the twelve tribes was selected. The twelve came back to give their findings, and there were two reports. The minority report, a faith report, came from Joshua and Caleb, "We can take the land because God has given it to us" (see Num. 13:30). The majority report said, "We can't take this land. There are fierce warriors and fortified cities and we are like grasshoppers in their sight" (Num. 13:32–33).

Unfortunately, the people listened to the grasshopper report of the majority. It cost them another forty years in the wilderness until that entire faithless generation had passed away. An entire generation—except for Joshua and Caleb—missed the Promised Land because of the grasshopper recordings that played in their heads. Where did those recordings come from? From four hundred years of being slaves in Egypt! Four hundred years of abuse and oppression. Four hundred years of seeing themselves as nobodies. Now they just couldn't see themselves as conquerors, even though God said that is what He had called them to be! (See Joshua 1.)

Fast-forward forty-five years to Joshua 17. A new generation of Israelites has entered into the Promised Land. They have experienced victory after victory as God had promised them. Jericho has fallen. Ai has fallen. A coalition of five kings has fallen before them, and on and on. There was still territory in the land that had not been conquered, but God said it was time to divide the land among the twelve tribes. The plan was to give each tribe their inheritance and then that tribe was to go in and drive out the inhabitants from their portion of the land. That story begins in Joshua 13 and following. What happens is both tragic and telling. Most of the tribes failed to drive the inhabitants out of the land as God had instructed. They failed to fully possess what God had promised to them. Why?

Because of the grasshopper recording that was still playing in their heads. In Joshua 17, the tribe of Manasseh comes back to Joshua to request more land than what was given to them. The reason they give for their request is that the Canaanites who live in the valleys of their land "have chariots of iron" (ı other words, "We can't drive them out as God said to do they have weapons of war." We are grasshoppers. Mos ...ᴜ people were never able to overcome that grasshopper recording, and the result was tragic. God had instructed them to drive the inhabitants out of the land completely so that His people would not be drawn away by the idols of the Canaanites. Because the Israelites did not drive the Canaanites out, that is exactly what happened all through the future of Israel. They were drawn after other gods.

Eventually the twelve tribes split into two kingdoms (1 Kings 12). The Northern Kingdom consisted of ten tribes and the Southern Kingdom consisted of two tribes. The North's rebellion and idolatry got so bad that God eventually withdrew his protecting hand from them. In 722 B.C., the Assyrians came against the Northern Kingdom and wiped them out. The Assyrians carried most of the people off into captivity. Then, in 586 B.C., the same happened with the Southern Kingdom, although this time the Babylonians did the sacking.

So a new generation of Israel, both kingdoms, ended up captives all over again because they were never able to break the mind-set that captives were all they were destined to be. That lie began with four hundred years of suffering and slavery in Egypt and followed them for centuries afterward. That is the power of a pattern of thinking about oneself. When the thinking is negative and the result of damaging experiences, the effects can be devastating.

### Change requires that we replace the lies with the truth

After Romans 12:2 says that we are to stop being conformed to this world, then the Scripture gives a positive command, "be transformed by the renewing of your mind." This is really good stuff. The word *transformed* is one of the great words of hope in the Bible, right alongside *grace* and *forgiveness*. In the original language it is the Greek word from which we get our word *metamorphosis*. In sophomore biology, most of us were introduced to the process that the caterpillar goes through inside its cocoon.

When it comes out, it has been transformed into a butterfly. That's a metamorphosis.

Verse 2 says that this process of transformation happens by the renewing of the mind. Here we get to the crux of the issue of change. We live in a world where we are constantly being squeezed into conformity to the world and its destructive recordings. The Enemy, the god of this world, uses everything at his disposal to force us into destructive patterns of thinking about ourselves, others, and about God. Hurtful, emotionally damaging experiences in life contribute to and reinforce these ways of thinking. Once these recordings become ingrained in our minds, we begin to live according to those thought patterns. Since conforming to the world begins in the mind, then transformation must also take place in our minds. Proverbs 23:7 says, "As he thinks within himself, so he is." In other words, we become what we think. If what we are doing needs to change, then what we are thinking must first be changed. Changed behavior will follow.

Second Corinthians 10:3–5 gives us a very practical and clear picture of why this change of beliefs is so difficult. The image used here is not one of being conformed and transformed, but of warfare, weapons, fortresses, and thoughts:

> For though we walk in the flesh, we do not war according to the flesh, for the weapons of our warfare are not of the flesh, but divinely powerful for the destruction of fortresses. We are destroying speculations and every lofty thing raised up against the knowledge of God, and we are taking every thought captive to the obedience of Christ.

The war, according to Romans 12, is between being conformed to the world and being transformed by the renewing of the mind. In 2 Corinthians 10, the war imagery is fully developed because there are weapons involved, there are fortresses that are built and have to come down, and there is an enemy that must be defeated. In fact, verse 4 says that our weapons are powerful for the destruction of fortresses.

What are these fortresses? Well, verse 5 indicates that they are fortresses of the mind. It says that speculations are being destroyed and "we are taking every thought captive to the obedience of Christ." These fortresses are fortresses of thought.

I don't want to take liberty with the text and make it say something that it does not say, but I want to make a practical application of this text to what the Hospital Church seeks to facilitate in people's lives. Please follow the logic with me:

Whenever we allow a thought to be conformed to the world—when we buy a lie of the Enemy about ourselves, others, or God—it is as if a brick is laid down in our mind. Another lie is believed, and another brick is laid down. On and on the process goes, until enough of the lies have been believed that a fortress has been constructed in our minds brick by brick. Then we are held captive by that fortress.

Or we can return to the imagery of the recording in our minds. It plays over and over and over and ultimately guides and directs our actions. It may be that because of hurtful and damaging experiences in life we come to believe that we are not a person of worth and value. That is a lie of the Enemy. We are, in fact, creations of God. But over time, brick by brick, that lie is reinforced until it becomes the defining value of our lives. It guides and directs every decision we make, impacts every relationship we enter, and colors our entire view of ourselves and our lives.

The emotional healing ministry of a hospital church is all about helping people go back and discover where those lies began, reveal them for the lies that they are, and then brick by brick begin to bring that fortress down. That is accomplished by "taking every thought captive to the obedience of Christ" (2 Cor. 10:5). Tearing fortresses down is a process that happens over time. Fortresses don't go up overnight, and they won't come down overnight either. But as we renew our mind and replace the lie of the Enemy about ourselves with the truth of God, fortresses will be torn down and captives will be set free!

## THE POWER OF WHAT WE BELIEVE

Allow me to go one step further in explaining why the mind must be renewed in order for real life transformation to happen.

I thank the men in my Saturday morning freedom group for being a sounding board where these thoughts could be hammered out.

One Saturday we were discussing the second step of the famed twelve steps of AA.[5] It states, "[We] came to believe that a Power greater than ourselves could restore us to sanity." That follows after the first step, which states, "We admitted we were powerless over [fill in the blank]—that our lives had become unmanageable." We discussed that when we admit our powerlessness within ourselves, that opens the door to begin looking outside of ourselves for a power greater than ourselves to make life work. That Power is Christ.

That's why the second step begins with "Came to believe." We have to stop believing the lie that we have the power to manage our lives. We must look to God's power. But to do that we have to "come to believe." Why? Because everything we do in life springs out of belief. What we become, what we do, is the result of our beliefs.

Once again, Proverbs 23:7, speaking of mankind, says, "As he thinks within himself, so he is." We become or act out of what we believe. As long as we hold on to the belief that we have the power within ourselves to make life work, we will keep trying to do it on our own. We have to abandon that belief—step one. And then come to a new belief that God is able to do what we have proven we cannot do effectively. That's step two.

The discussion with my small group that Saturday morning prompted me to ask the men a question. "Is it possible to act contrary to what you believe?" The response was almost immediate from the guys. Heads started shaking "yes" all over the room. That is, except for those who smelled a trick question. They stayed very stoic and noncommittal.

Then I said, "No, I don't believe it is possible." There were groans and murmurs all over the room. I thought I was about to be tarred and feathered and carried out of town on a pole. So I

---

5. See "The Twelve Steps of Alcoholics Anonymous," rev. 5/9/02, A.A. World Services, Inc., http://www.aa.org/en_pdfs/smf-121_en.pdf.

quickly went on to say, "It is possible to act contrary to what you *say* you believe, or what you *think* you believe, or what you have *convinced* yourself that you believe, but not what you *really* believe." Now they were settling down a little and willing to at least discuss the issue. I was safe for the time being, but I had to speak quickly before the mob rose up again to do me bodily harm. So I spoke about golf:

If you are a golfer who typically shoots 95 as an average score, you are eventually going to want to improve that score, particularly if your regular foursome is made up of three other guys who typically shoot 85.

Now, anyone who plays golf knows that the only way to take ten strokes off your score is to change your golf swing. You have to learn to hit the ball straighter. So you decide to go to a swing coach to see what is wrong with your swing. The instructor takes a look at your swing and says something like, "Well I can see that you are laying the club off at the top of the backswing, and that is causing you to come over the top on the downswing. That's why you hit that big old slice into the trees." So he helps you get your swing on plane on the backswing so it will come back down on plane and strike the ball more solidly and more squarely at impact.

You are pumped now. This is exactly what you have been wanting. So next Saturday you meet up with your playing buddies, and you tell them about how everything is going to be different today because you got a lesson and have figured this thing out.

But at the end of the day you don't shoot 85. You shoot 105! Your buddies really talk trash afterward as you sit in the nineteenth hole reviewing the round.

So you go to the driving range some that week and try to work on the new swing. The next Saturday you go out with your foursome and shoot over 100 again. After a few weeks of this, the abuse you are taking from the guys is more than you can stand, and you are completely mystified and frustrated. You think to yourself, "I thought my game was supposed to get better with this new swing! But I'm worse than I ever was." You have entered what's known as the "valley of despair." What you do next is critical to what kind of long-term results you get.

Truthfully, most golfers can't stay in this valley very long. What most do is abandon the swing changes and go back to the old swing that produced a 95 score for them. But that isn't all they do. They don't just go back to the old swing, but they also "try harder" at it. And nothing changes.

The problem is, if you are doing the wrong thing, trying harder at it won't bring a better result. So, six months later you are frustrated again with your 95 score and you go back to the swing coach. The coach says, "Well I haven't got anything different to tell you today than I told you six months ago." So you start the cycle all over again. You try the same new swing for a while, abandon it, go back to the old and try harder at it, get frustrated, go to the swing coach, hear the same thing again, over and over, blah, blah, blah.

Here's a truth: in any kind of change, whether golf or life, it usually gets worse for a while before it gets better. There is almost always a "valley of despair" that has to be walked through. You have to stay in the valley long enough to allow your swing changes to become comfortable before you begin to see the benefit from them. To do that, you have to do two things. First, you have to abandon the old belief that you can work harder with your faulty swing and get the result that you want. Second, you have adopt the new belief that the new swing is the way to an 85 score and that if you keep doing it you will eventually get there. This new belief, if you really believe it, will give you the courage to stay in the valley as long as it takes to get the positive change you desire.

Change in golf has to begin with belief. Change in life is no different. I have to abandon my faulty beliefs that imprison me to my destructive behavior, and adopt new beliefs that are going to result in healthy behavior. It is the renewing of the mind that Romans 12:2 talks about.

This same principle I've illustrated with the golfer can also be seen in the life of a recovering addict who periodically acts out in his addiction. If you ask her if she believes that it is ever good for her to act out in her addiction, she will probably tell you "no, it is never good." But she doesn't really believe that.

She wants to believe that, she knows she should believe it, and she has even convinced herself that she does believe it. But that isn't what she *really* believes. If it were, she would never act out in her addiction.

In fact, in those moments when she is taking the steps that will ultimately lead her to acting out, her true belief is that there is going to be some good for her from acting out. She will get a short-term relief from whatever is stressing her out or troubling her. She "believes" that it is good to get that temporary relief. No matter what she may claim to believe, her actions show that she hasn't completely abandoned the faulty belief that there is some benefit that can come from acting out. Once she truly abandons that old faulty belief and adopts the new belief that complete sobriety is always best for her, she will begin to live in total sobriety.

One of the things that we lead people to do in the Hospital Church is to take a look at their actions that they know need to change and trace them back to the belief upon which those actions are based. If the action is contradictory to the belief, then they need to begin to dig beneath what they "think" they believe and get to the real, faulty belief that is underneath. It's like stripping the layers of paint off an old piece of furniture to find the original color. You keep peeling off the layers of denial and self-deception until you get down to the core of what you really believe. When that is recognized for what it is, then you can begin the process of renewing the mind in that area and experience the victory of changed behavior. Here is a guiding principle that we teach everyone in the Hospital Church. "If your conviction (belief) isn't reflected in your behavior, it is not a conviction but a contradiction. Contradictions always indicate a deception."

I'm convinced that Christians say we believe a lot of things that we don't really believe. We say we believe these things because we know we should believe them, and we would like to believe them, but that is all just a cover for what we really believe. For instance, if I say I believe that God wants to guide my daily life, but I never seek His guidance, do I really believe He wants to guide me? When a belief changes, everything changes with it. That's how real change happens.

## HOPE FOR TODAY

On a Sunday afternoon in the summer of 2001, I got a call at my home. A man named Brad was on the other end. He was sitting in the parking lot of our church speaking to me on his cell phone, about to take his own life.

I had never met Brad. I had no idea who he was. Someone had given him my home phone number. To this day I do not know who. Brad was desperate, so I agreed to meet him at a restaurant immediately. We met for several hours, and Brad told me about himself.

Brad was near fifty. He held a responsible job with a large commercial electrical contracting company. He also was a desperate alcoholic and cocaine addict. The addictive spiral had gotten so tight and was spinning so fast that his life had finally spun out of control. Brad believed that there was no hope for him. He had convinced himself that things would be best if his life just ended—a major lie of the Enemy, but a fortress had been built in his mind.

I began to share with Brad that there was hope in Jesus Christ. There was hope that he could be free from his despair. He asked me how, and I shared the gospel with him. When I had finished, Brad said that he wanted to accept Christ as his Savior right then and there. He bowed his head and heart in his desperation and in submission to Christ as Savior.

Afterward, I told him that this was the most important step he could ever take, but it wasn't the end. It was the beginning. Now there was a war to be fought. His body needed to be free from the chemicals, and his mind had to be set free from the lies. Christ would set him free, but both freedoms were going to come through a process that would include being involved in loving accountability, an infusion of the truth of God to replace the lies that he had lived with all of his life, and some plain old tough decisions that he was going to have to make.

Brad soon entered a treatment center for detox and spent the next thirty days there. Afterward, he became immersed in the Hospital Church ministry, as well as regular meetings with a Narcotics Anonymous group in which he is still active. I had lunch with Brad recently. We reminisced about that day we met at the restaurant. As we talked, tears welled up in Brad's eyes. What a change from that day. He is celebrating five years in Christ and five years without drugs or alcohol. He has become a leader in helping others find hope from addiction and hope in Christ. He speaks at conferences around the state and mentors others who are struggling with addictive and destructive behaviors.

What a great and mighty God we serve. What a privilege to pastor a hospital church ministry where people like Brad are not only received but welcomed. A place where lies can be revealed for what they are and replaced with truth, where people can experience true and lasting change.

CHAPTER 7

# COMMUNITY:
# THE ONE-ANOTHER PROCESS

For almost two years I put off writing this chapter. In fact, the manuscript for the rest of the book was virtually finished before I could bring myself to sit down and begin writing it. My hesitation wasn't from a lack of knowledge about small groups, cell groups, community groups, or any number of names they are called by. In fact, my doctoral thesis was on the subject of small groups. In the preparation and writing of that thesis, I read virtually everything in print at the time about small groups. Over the next twenty years, I led my church into an extensive small group ministry. We encourage everyone in the body to be a part of a community group, because I do believe that good things happen in small groups, as the title of one well-known book on the subject proclaims. I knew what prompted my hesitation about writing this chapter—I had something fresh to say about the subject, but I just couldn't find a framework for the words.

Then, in March 2008, I was on a trip to Laredo, Texas, to watch my son play one of his last college golf tournaments before turning professional. As is often the case while I am on the road, my mind began to mull over the subject of small groups and the problem I was having writing this chapter. Similar to how I developed the framework for the Pile Principle, the answer I was looking for came while zooming along the interstate. Unfortunately, I was on my Harley Davidson this time, so I couldn't steer with my knee while taking notes. I was so excited I pulled off the freeway to the parking lot of a fast-food restaurant and wrote the ideas for this chapter down.

Later, back in my office, I fleshed out the new paradigm. Most of the literature written for the church about small groups focuses on believers getting connected together in relationships and doing life together. I am certainly for that! We practice that kind of relational-oriented small group experience at the Hospital Church. But I wanted to write about a paradigm for small groups that focuses on "from the ground up" life transformation—the kind of small group where chaos and addictions can be addressed honestly, where complete and total transparency can be practiced, where toenail-curling honesty is the norm, where no secrets are kept, and where biblical tools for changing lifelong patterns of destructive attitudes and behaviors can be learned and practiced in a supportive yet accountable environment. That's the type of small groups I espouse.

This paradigm for small groups is what fires me up today and is the key missing link in the majority of small group ministries of today's average church. I, and many others in hospital church ministries, have experienced these small groups, and once you've experienced this paradigm you don't know how you could live without it. I certainly don't. If I had to put my mask back on and guard my heart as I did for so many years, I don't think I could go forward. Once you have experienced true biblical fellowship, and the change that happens in that context, all the substitutes for fellowship lose their attraction.

I realize I've made some strong statements here, and if you're a pastor who oversees a small group ministry, or if you have small groups at your church, I don't mean this as a criticism of what you're doing. I mean this as an invitation. Maybe you've never been taught that small groups can become more than relational-oriented. Or perhaps your church's small group ministry places a strong emphasis on evangelism as the focus for your groups—this focus is not wrong by any means, but it does define and sometimes even limit the groups' depth. Or perhaps you've dreamed for a long time about small groups that help facilitate life change becoming the true backbone in your church—you've glimpsed these groups in action, but only in snippets.

I invite you to consider a new type of small group. These small groups form the core structure of any hospital church ministry. Specifically, they provide the foundational platform for the emotional-and-spiritual healing ministry of our church, and churches just like ours. But these types of small groups may well be small groups like you've never seen before. We don't even call them small groups at our church. Our core, life-transformational groups are called freedom groups. We also have a separate structure of small groups at our church called community groups, which look and act similar to traditional small groups—they are intentionally relational and ministry focused. But our freedom groups have a completely different focus and purpose.

## ONE ANOTHER

Anyone who has studied the Bible is familiar with the "one another" statements. I have referred to them many times over the years and taught through most of the passages. One thing I had never done before writing this chapter was put all of them down together. When you see them all lined up next to each other, the impact is powerful. I won't list all of them because most of them are stated more than once. A few of them such as "love one another" are stated many times over. Let me just line them up and let them speak:

- Wash one another's feet (John 13:14).

- Love one another, as Christ has loved you (John 13:34).

- Be devoted to one another, give preference to one another (Rom. 12:10).

- Be of the same mind toward one another (Rom. 12:16).

- Do not judge one another (Rom. 14:13).

- Pursue things that build one another up (Rom. 14:19).

- Accept one another (Rom. 15:7).

- Bear one another's burdens (Gal. 6:2).

- Show tolerance to one another (Eph. 4:2).

- Speak truth to one another in love (Eph. 4:15, 25).

- Be kind to one another, forgive one another (Eph. 4:32).

- Be subject to one another (Eph. 5:21).

- Regard one another as more important than yourselves (Phil. 2:3).

- Do not lie to one another (Col. 3:9).

- Bear with one another (Col. 3:13).

- With wisdom teach and admonish one another (Col. 3:16).

- Comfort one another (1 Thess. 4:18).

- Encourage and build up one another (1 Thess. 5:11).

- Live in peace with one another (1 Thess. 5:13).

- Stimulate one another to love and good deeds (Heb. 10:24).

- Confess your sins to one another and pray for one another (James 5:16).

- Be hospitable to one another (1 Peter 4:9).

- Serve one another (1 Peter 4:10).

- Clothe yourselves with humility toward one another (1 Peter 5:5).

That biblical foundation of "one anotherness" is the essence of our freedom groups.

God doesn't do His healing work in isolation but in community. Life is made up of relationships, pure and simple. When relationships are good, life is good. When relationships are bad, life is bad. As we saw in chapter 4, spiritual maturity is about an intimate relationship with God; emotional maturity is about intimate relationships with others. But emotional wounds prevent intimacy and hinder maturity. The vast majority of our emotionally wounding experiences have come from people. It only makes sense that God would use people to bring healing to those emotional wounds. In other words, if life is relationships, and emotional wounds hinder our ability to fully experience relationships, it only makes logical sense that God would use relationships to bring the emotional healing that is needed for life's relationships.

This is why I never advise someone to seek counseling by itself but recommend the freedom group process along with counseling. Counseling is an artificial, professional relationship. You see a counselor for perhaps an hour per week, you are paying for that hour, and the counselor knows only what you tell him or her. The freedom group is a people-to-people process where relationships of accountability are established that are available all during the week, and you can't fool a fooler. People in a freedom group can smell a cover-up from a mile away because most of them have been practitioners of the cover-up at some time or other. In every good freedom group there are those who have moved beyond the cover-up and can gently and lovingly help the fooler drop the mask. It's all done in relationship. This process is particularly powerful when it is practiced in the context of the body of Christ.

Most of the freedom groups at the Hospital Church have a life cycle of twelve to sixteen weeks. During that time, people share their deepest fears, hurts, and resentments with one another along with confessions of behaviors that often have not been spoken of openly before. They encourage one another to practice the tools of transformation they are learning in the group. When it's over, there are bonds that have been forged on the anvil of honesty and transparency that never go away. When these people see each other on Sunday morning they realize that they "know" and are "known" on a level that is rarely achieved in any church. When they are together in a Bible study class or a community small group, there is a depth to their knowledge of each other that can't be achieved any other way. Over the course of time, when a person has been in several groups, either as a member or as a facilitator of the group, their circle of people that they "know" and are "known by" is ever increasing.

That kind of intimacy isn't something that can be achieved in a traditional small group, or our community groups as we call them, nor would it be appropriate to attempt there. The typical community group isn't designed for that, nor is it equipped to deal with the issues that often arise and are addressed in a freedom group. What a community group can provide is another venue where the person who is experiencing emotional healing can practice the principles that he or she is learning in the freedom group process.

One of the saddest statements I have ever heard from Christians in recovery outside of their church is, "I have a deeper level of transparency and honesty with the unbelievers in my recovery group outside of my church than I could ever have with people in my church. The people in my church simply don't get it and wouldn't know what to do with the kinds of things we deal with in my recovery group." Many Christians in recovery from addictions or emotional wounds have simply resolved themselves to this contradiction as a fact of life. It is more often than not a fact of reality about the church. But it is a very sad fact of reality.

## THE PROBLEM WITH SMALL GROUPS

I know that my statement about the limits of transparency and honesty that can be achieved, or would even be appropriate to attempt to achieve, in a community group, are controversial statements to some. If you have put all of your eggs of transparency and honesty in the community group basket, then to admit its limitations can be a difficult thing to do. But there are limitations.

Consider Tom, a man who has a strong addiction to pornography. Where would Tom find help? From his typical small group? Perhaps from a men's Bible study? What the men in that group would probably say to Tom if he shared this need is something like, "We'll pray for you, brother, but you need to go get counseling for that."

That's the problem. A promise to pray is an easy answer to give, and what is perceived as the "real" help is supposedly found outside the church. That shouldn't be the case, and in a hospital church ministry, it isn't.

Here's another scenario. Tammy has been sexually abused, either as a child, adolescent, or adult. She, like a majority of people in this situation, has never told anyone or experienced any healing of those wounds. The effects of this trauma are creeping up on her. Tammy wants to unload the burden. Where does she find help? Would the typical mixed-gender community group be an appropriate place for her to share that experience and receive the real healing she needs? Certainly the people in her community group would feel compassion for her and pray for her, but would they be equipped to walk Tammy through the process of healing and recovery that she needs? I doubt it. They'd probably refer her to outside counsel.

Some churches that are large enough might provide a counselor on staff. Typically, the client still has to pay something for the counseling to cover the cost of the counselor to the church. But whether or not it costs something, there we are again, back in the artificial relationship situation. I could go on and on about scenarios where community groups are just not enough.

In the Hospital Church, we don't have to refer anyone outside the church to get help. We recognize that all the principles of recovery and healing are right there in the Word of God and that it is the calling of the body of Christ to be a place where help can be found. Help is found right there in the relationships. No need to go anywhere but the body of Jesus for help and healing.

Now that I am deep into controversial statements, let me make another: For a church to provide small groups and not provide freedom groups can be counterproductive, and even dangerous.

The typical call of the average church is, "Hey, come be a part of a small group." It's an open-arms invitation for anybody and everybody to show up and join and build relationships. But the prime place where emotional wounds show up, and thus have the most damaging effect, is in relationships. Remember: everyone has some level of emotional woundedness, we are all wounded by sin and the fall, and some of us have been wounded deeply. So we put people in small groups for them to develop meaningful, intimate relationships. But what a small group often amounts to (in terms of the Pile Principle) is a group of people bringing their individual piles of emotional garbage and stacking them all together in the middle of the room into one giant heap of garbage. The group stinks, but nobody can really figure out why! So week after week the group meets, trying to develop community because they know that's what they are there for, but they're never able to achieve it. There are relationship conflicts that aren't resolved, hurt feelings, lack of trust, resentments, and on the list goes. These continue to build up as normal people interact with each other, until the group implodes upon itself or until, to everyone's relief, the small group coordinator disbands the group. Many people from that group will never become a part of another community group. They say, "Been there, done that, and don't need the aggravation."

Whenever we give an open-arms invitation for everybody to join small groups, we are setting people up for failure and then wondering why they failed. We put them into small groups to develop intimacy that is beyond what they are capable of developing at their level of emotional maturity, and then wonder why it didn't happen.

Perhaps most of the people in a community group are at a level of emotional health where they are able to function well in that environment and achieve some meaningful community. But there are always one or two people in a group who are what is called in small group parlance EGR people: Extra Grace Required. These are people that can suck the life out of the group. They are the proverbial square pegs in round holes, the flat tires on the bus. They just don't function well in a small group. Why? Because they aren't emotionally healthy enough to do so.

People must have some minimum level of emotional health to be able to be a contributing member of a small group experience. Until they are at that level, all they can do is drain the small group.

What does grace really look like in a situation with an EGR person in your small group? Put up with the person in the group? Feel sorry for him? Tolerate her? Silently dread going to group? Let this couple continue to suck the life out of the group until the group implodes?

No. What EGR people need isn't just extra grace but emotional healing. Grace in that situation makes sure they can get the healing they need so they can eventually give and receive that kind of fellowship. And that's what freedom groups are designed for.

In the Hospital Church, we have an extensive community group ministry. Our community group leaders know that sometimes they need to go to an EGR person and lovingly, gently, yet firmly recommend that the person access a freedom group first in order to experience some emotional healing in an area where it is needed. This isn't a particularly insulting suggestion, since freedom groups are such an integral part of the Hospital Church, and we recommend that everyone be a part of the groups anyway.

It's key that we don't present freedom groups as something that is only for those "sickos and addicts, and not for all us regular folks." Freedom groups are for everybody wounded by the fall, and it is important to make this clear to everyone within the church. I am a part of a freedom group and I am the senior pastor of the church.

## THE BEGINNING OF HEALING

The Bible teaches what seems, to many people, to be a contradiction. In the world system, the way up is up. You keep moving up the ladder, looking out for number one, even stepping on others if you need to. But in the kingdom of God the way up is down, and the way down is up. Humility leads to glory. From God's perspective, as long as I am scrambling to scratch my way up to the top, I am eventually going to be brought down. When I give up trying to scratch my way up and instead bow down, then He will raise me up in His time (James 4:10).

That is the essence of Jesus' statement that He repeated several times to His disciples. Matthew 23:11–12 says, "But the greatest among you shall be your servant. Whoever exalts himself shall be humbled; and whoever humbles himself shall be exalted." Christ, the greatest among us, was also the greatest servant. Although He is the Lord of glory, He washed the disciples' feet (John 13:5). And Paul says about Christ in Philippians 2:8, "He humbled Himself . . . to the point of death, even death on a cross."

Let's look at a few passage to get a feel for how God feels about pride.

Proverbs 6:16–17 says, "There are six things which the LORD hates, yes, seven which are an abomination to Him: haughty eyes. . . ." Haughty eyes can be translated "a proud look" (e.g., NKJV). It is the first in God's list of seven things He hates.

Proverbs 15:25 says, "The LORD will tear down the house of the proud." Now, if the house being spoken of here was brick and mortar, that would be serious enough. But the house in this context represents a man's life.

Proverbs 16:5 says, "Everyone who is proud in heart is an abomination to the LORD." *Abomination* is a strong word. It means something that is immeasurably abhorrent and detestable. The heart of pride is a thing of horror to God.

Isaiah 13:11 says, "Thus I will punish the world for its evil and the wicked for their iniquity; I will also put an end to the arrogance of the proud." God is saying here, "I'm done with it! I'm going to put an end to it. I'm not going to tolerate it anymore!"

Pride is at the top of God's list of things that He hates and will not tolerate. One of my favorite movies of all time is the television miniseries from the 1990s, *Lonesome Dove*. It's the story of two retired Texas Rangers who lead a cattle drive from South Texas all the way into Montana. Robert Duvall plays Gus, and Tommy Lee Jones plays Captain Woodrow Call. In one scene the drive has arrived at a town, so all the drovers go into town for supplies. Call comes upon a fellow who was beating up on one of his young drovers. Call gets off his horse and beats the stuffing out of the bully. It's a hard scene to watch, even though you know it is only acting. Afterward, Call gets up on his horse and delivers this classic line: "I can't stand rude behavior in a man. I won't tolerate it." About once a year I go back and watch all six hours of the miniseries on DVD. Every time I come to that part I think, "That's how God feels about pride." He says, "I can't stand pride in a man. I won't tolerate it." Pride blocks everything that God wants to do in our lives. He's dedicated to putting an end to it.

Finally, James 4:6 says, "God is opposed to the proud, but gives grace to the humble." That pretty much sums up everything that God's Word says about pride and humility. He hates one and blesses the other. The real impact of what the Bible says about God's attitude toward pride, which is summed up in this verse, is that God isn't neutral when it comes to our pride. He is actively working in opposition to it. He opposes us in our pride!

## PRIDE'S SUBTLETY

When I was a kid growing up in West Texas, football was king. Like everyone in my hometown, I played football, beginning in junior high. I was a wing back, a running back. I wasn't very big, but I could run like a jackrabbit. Our team was good, and we knew it. Through the seventh and eighth grade we were undefeated in our district. We strutted around and talked smack like we were the Dallas Cowboys.

One day our coach, Coach Bob—who walked with a limp and was mean as a snake—scheduled a practice game against the junior varsity team from Pecos. They were ninth and tenth graders. I'm telling you, these guys had beards and mustaches! I'm sure some of them were married, had kids, and held jobs. They were huge.

We got in the huddle for the first play, and our quarterback, Pat Rodriguez (Pat Rod), called the first play. I remember it to this day. Tight X right 224 on set. It meant I was to carry the ball right through to the left of the center. I looked at Pat Rod and said, "Are you kiddin' me? The first play?" He looked at me with an evil grin and said, "That's right." So we lined up. I was right behind the quarterback in the I formation. When I looked across to the defense, where I was about to carry the ball, I saw a linebacker who'd already done time in the state penitentiary and had come back to finish the ninth grade! When Pat Rod handed me the ball, I didn't even get to the line of scrimmage. That guy leveled our offensive lineman, caught me in the back field, and spiked me head first into the ground. When I got up, I had grass stuck in my face mask, and I was looking out the ear hole of my helmet. I staggered back to the huddle and said, "Pat Rod, you give Woodall the ball this time. I don't want it." The other team strummed us that day. We didn't talk much smack after that. Coach Bob in his infinite wisdom had known we needed a good lesson in humility.

The point? Whenever we choose to walk in our pride, God lines up against us like that linebacker. God opposes the proud and gives grace to the humble, just like James 4:6 says.

Humility is the beginning place of all help, hope, and healing that comes from God. The founders of Alcoholics Anonymous understood that. It's no accident that the first step is about humility. They didn't just figure it out; they got it right from Scripture. These men were actively involved in Bible study, and they consulted ministers as they developed the twelve steps.[1] In

1. Bill Pittman with Dick B., *Courage to Change: The Christian Roots of the Twelve-Step Movement* (Center City, MN: Hazelden, 1998), 11–24.

the first step you have to name the problem and admit defeat! I can't overcome this on my own. The first step says, "We admitted that we were powerless over alcohol—that our lives had become unmanageable."[2] If alcohol isn't your problem, you can fill in the blank with whatever you need to: We admitted that we were powerless over control; fear; selfishness; insecurity; sex; food; deception; and on and on.

Jesus spoke of humility this way in the first beatitude: "Blessed are the poor in spirit, for theirs is the kingdom of heaven" (Matt. 5:3). The word *poor* in the original language doesn't mean you're out of change for a mocha. It's a word that means total and complete destitution! Completely empty. Impoverished. I've got nothing with which to present myself to God. I've got nothing to brag about, take credit for, or be proud of that is in my flesh. When you admit that, what do you get? The kingdom of heaven. When you admit you have nothing, Jesus says you get everything! As long as you still think you have something, you get nothing. God is the source of the emotional healing that we need. To get it we have to lose the pride and begin to walk in humility before Him and others. Humility is the key to everything that we need from God.

So what does this all have to do with the "one another" process lived out in freedom groups? The best way to explain the connection is to tell you a part of my own story. In the introduction, I shared some of my experience in the late eighties to early nineties when I spiraled down to a point of desperation. In that time I was memorizing entire books of the Bible, not just verses, and praying for hours on end for God to deliver me from the pain I was in, but I got nothing. No help came. It wasn't until I began to talk to others about my pain, as we transitioned the church into the Hospital Church format, that I began to experience healing. At the time I didn't get the connection. I was just thankful to be coming out of the hole I was in.

The light was more fully turned on for me when I went through a Bible-based twelve-step process. The second step

---

2. See "The Twelve Steps of Alcoholics Anonymous," rev. 5/9/02, A.A. World Services, Inc., http://www.aa.org/en_pdfs/smf-121_en.pdf.

says, "We came to believe that a power greater than ourselves could restore us to sanity." In that workbook, *The Twelve Steps, A Spiritual Journey*, the very first instruction in the second step chapter is, "List some of the experiences that caused you to lose faith in God."[3] The first time I was confronted with that instruction, I was offended by it. I thought, "I never lost faith in God." The thought was so offensive to me that I couldn't even consider it at the time. I was a Christian, I had three theological degrees, I was a pastor. I loved Jesus. I never lost faith in God. But I had to write something so I will give it to you exactly as I wrote it: "In the early nineties I was praying and seeking God with all that was in me but continued to spiral down. I didn't lose faith, but it hurt."

Then I went on. Over the next months I eventually completed the twelve-step workbook, and then our group started all over again at the beginning. I have learned that the twelve-step journey isn't something you just do and then you are done. It is a lifestyle that you live over and over, and every time you do it, it's like peeling another layer off the onion. Each layer you get a little closer to the core.

When I came to that instruction in the second chapter this time around, I read what I had written and I immediately thought, "That's a crock! I can't believe I actually wrote that!" You see, by this time I had cut through the denial to the extent that I was able to admit that I really had been upset with God that He didn't pull me out of that darkness when I was crying out to Him. As I looked at this question this time it dawned on me that I still felt upset. I still didn't understand why He hadn't rescued me when I was crying out to Him.

This second time through the workbook, I still had to answer all the questions, but once again I didn't know what to write for this one. So I did what we tell people to do in that situation. We say, "Put your pen on the paper, start writing and ask God to guide your pen." He guided my pen, and this is word for word what I wrote: "I have since come to understand that God wasn't

---

3. *The Twelve Steps, A Spiritual Journey*, rev. ed. (San Diego: RPI, 1994), 45. I have since written my on biblically based twelve-step workbook.

ignoring me or rejecting me. I was still trying to get through it in my own power without humbling myself to others. Sometimes our reaching out to God is not faith but an expression of our pride. We don't want to humble ourselves before others, so we try to do it in secret, just between God and me." I stared at that statement dumbfounded.

What I realized that instant was that all of what I had been doing during that time of pain—crying out to God, memorizing Scripture by books—all that I was calling faith, He was calling pride. You see, I didn't want to let anyone else know what was going on inside of me, and that was my pride. So, I tried to get it all fixed up just between me and God, so nobody else would ever know. He was in essence saying to me, "Son, I love you and I want to lift you up, but I have to resist you in your pride. If I helped you now I would only be supporting you in your pride. I love you but I hate your pride." Like that linebacker from Pecos, God was across the line of scrimmage to oppose me, because I was so full of myself.

When I look back over how the healing process has taken place in my life, I realize that it began when I quit just crying out to God and started swallowing my pride enough to talk to other people about it. Then my heavenly Father said, "Now I can enter into the process with you and for you." Now that I understand that truth, I never want to hide, keep secrets, or walk in that kind of pride again. That is why I stay in the process of freedom groups. I can mark it down as pretty much a forgone conclusion that anytime now there is an issue in my life that I seem to be unable to get victory over, the basic problem almost always comes back to some root of pride in me. When I see it for what it is, address it, and confess it before God and others, that is when the breakthrough always begins.

The fifth step of alcoholics anonymous addresses this issue. The fourth step is when we take a "searching and fearless moral inventory."[4] Every wrong act, attitude, destructive behavior, we

---

4. See "The Twelve Steps of Alcoholics Anonymous," rev. 5/9/02, A.A. World Services, Inc., http://www.aa.org/en_pdfs/smf-121_en.pdf.

put it down on paper and see it for what it is. Then, in step five we, "Admitted to God, to ourselves, and to another human being the exact nature of our wrongs."[5] That is a part of the humbling process. It is also very biblical. We are told in Scripture to confess our sins to God, but we are also instructed to confess our sins to one another (James 5:16). I find that the more I am willing to allow others to see and hear my confession, the more freedom I gain from what is imprisoning me.

The freedom group structure provides a safe place, a safe venue to begin learning to live with that kind of openness and humility. It provides a safe place to experience the joy and freedom that living without secrets can bring. It is designed and structured specifically for that purpose unlike any other small group experience.

## WHOLENESS THROUGH HELPING

Wholeness is when you come to the place where you can give more than you have to receive. We always need to receive because we will always need to be in the process of being changed. But wholeness means I can give away to others more than I have to receive. There are always new people coming into the process who are initially only receiving. That's okay in the beginning, but it isn't where we should stay. So there always needs to be people who are further into the process and able to pour back into the lives of others. This is a cycle of receiving help and then giving it away.

That is in fact the essence of the twelfth step. "Having had a spiritual awakening as the result of these Steps, we tried to carry this message to others, and to practice these principles in all our affairs."[6] A key part of the genius and success of AA over the decades is that people don't just come in, get help, and then quit. They stay in the process and sponsor others, giving from what they have received. They understand two key truths: there are people who need to hear of their experience, strength, and hope;

---

5. Ibid.
6. See "The Twelve Steps of Alcoholics Anonymous," rev. 5/9/02, A.A. World Services, Inc., http://www.aa.org/en_pdfs/smf-121_en.pdf.

and they need to keep giving it away in order to keep growing in the process themselves. You know you are really getting it when you are able and willing to give it away.

This again isn't something that the founders of AA thought up on their own. It's a principle of Jesus. Matthew 10:8 says, "freely you received, freely give." You can't give away what you don't have anymore than you can come back from someplace you've never been. But once you really have it, you can't keep from giving it away.

One of my favorite stories in the ministry of Jesus is recorded in Mark 2. Jesus is teaching in a house and the place is packed. It's so full that people are even stuffed into the doorway. Four guys show up carrying their friend who is paralyzed and on a pallet. They want to get him to Jesus in hopes that Jesus will heal him. They see the crowd packed in like sardines and immediately recognize this isn't going to be easy, but they aren't about to give up. They haul their buddy up on the flat roof of the house. Evidently they measure it all out and figure out just about where Jesus is sitting in the house. Right there they start destroying the roof. This roof would probably have been made of mud and straw, mixed together and baked in the sun. The friends start chipping away at the roof until they have a hole big enough to lower their friend through. I can imagine Jesus teaching, while bits and pieces of roof begin to rain down. Everything stops down below. All eyes are up on the ceiling. When the hole is big enough, these four faces peer down into the house to make sure they have estimated Jesus' position correctly. When they are sure they have it right, down comes their friend on a pallet, lowered right down in front of Jesus. Jesus is moved by their faith, and I think He also must have been moved by their love and commitment to their friend. He heals the paralytic. The guy picks up his pallet and walks out the front door.

Freely you received, freely give. If that man is going to honor and obey that principle, what is he going to do? Well, if he really grasps the magnitude of the gift he has received, he is going to find someone else who needs help and carry them up on the roof if need be, in order to get to Jesus. He's going to want to share the joy, the hope, and the healing. If he doesn't want to do that, it's an indication that he doesn't really comprehend the magnitude of the gift he has received.

You know you've really got it when you want to give it away. Freedom groups in the church provide a venue for people to get the emotional healing they need and then help others. Helped people never stop giving it away to others. That's why we call it the "one-another" process—you give to me and I give back to you. Together we give to others, and the gift keeps giving.

## THE POWER OF THE HERD

Not long ago someone encouraged me to watch a short video that had been put up on YouTube. Some people on a photographic safari in Africa witnessed something that wildlife photographers work their entire lives to capture on film. They were filming a pride of lions that were watching a herd of water buffalo. There was a little water buffalo at the edge of the herd that the lions had their eyes on. The lions began the chase and tackled the little water buffalo. They began gnawing his tough hide as he struggled to get away. In the struggle, they kept edging closer and closer to a water hole. Eventually the little buffalo fell down into the edge of the water. One of the lions had him by the head now, trying to drag him back up the bank. The buffalo's rear end is in the water. About that time a crocodile comes up out of the water and grabs him by the rear end. Now lions have him on one end and an alligator has him on the other end. Both are trying to have him for lunch. Somehow, the lions win the tug-of-war and get him back on land. They go to work on him again. You figure the buffalo's a goner.

Then an incredible thing happens. You see the herd of water buffalo rush back into the picture. They've figured something out. They are bigger than the lions, and there are more of them than lions, and they have these huge appendages on their heads called horns that can do major damage to lions. The lions don't seem to be very concerned. Then, one of the buffalos puts his horns to work and sends a lion ten feet in the air. Then the rest of the buffalos begin to move in on the lions. Suddenly the lions have to rethink whether this little water buffalo is worth the price. They decide that he isn't and start to get the heck out of Dodge. That stokes the herd even more, and as the video ends the lions are running away with their tails tucked between their legs with the water buffalo hot on their trail.

Miraculously, the little water buffalo stands up and runs back into the middle of the herd where he is safe. I'll bet he never lagged behind again. Watching that video you want to stand up and cheer! Yippee! The lions lost! The herd won! Yea for the herd! Yea for community!

There are so many applications that can be drawn from that video. But three come to mind that are particularly relevant to the topic of community. First, we are most vulnerable when we aren't connected to community. Second, there are multiple enemies out there waiting to take us down. The Bible identifies three of them: the world (Rom 12:2; 1 John 2:16), Satan (John 10:10; 1 Peter 5:8), and the flesh (Rom 7:14–25). The third, and most important application for this chapter is about the power of community to overcome.

In the video, I was struck by how tentative the herd was at first. They weren't sure of themselves. But by the end of the video, they were kicking lion butt and taking names. They realized they had the advantage and didn't need to be intimidated by lions. They had a size advantage, a toughness advantage, a strength advantage, and a numbers advantage. They could rescue their own.

I'm waiting for the body of Christ to wake up and realize that we have everything we need to rescue the hurting and wounded among us. We don't need to be intimidated. We don't need to look to the world to rescue our own. We have the indwelling Holy Spirit for power. We have the Word of God for the principles of healing and overcoming. We have one another for the process. We don't need to be intimidated. We don't need to be tentative. What we do need to be is serious about the process and aware about the need. I believe the first and greatest obstacle is gaining awareness.

As I talk about the hospital church ministry with church leaders, the level of denial I witness overwhelms me. They seem to think that their church doesn't have any great number of emotionally wounded people. They don't have that many people who struggle with addictions. They don't have that many women or men who have been scarred by sexual abuse. They don't have that many men who struggle with pornography or full-blown sexual addiction. "Freedom group ministry is fine for churches who have all of that," they say, "but it isn't something my church needs to do because we don't have those problems. The few in our church who do have problems, we just ship them off to a counselor or an AA group to get what they need."

What I always respond with is this: "If your church was a safe place for people to *admit* those struggles and hurts, and if you provided *real* help and hope for them, they would come out of the woodwork, and you would be shocked by who they are. They are in every tax bracket, every social bracket, and every educational bracket. They are elders, deacons, Sunday school teachers, ushers, greeters, staff members, small group leaders, worship team members, average church attendees, and guests who show up on Sunday morning. They are everywhere in your church. Maybe they are you."

That's why we need one another.

# CHAPTER 8

# TRANSPARENCY:
# THE HOSPITAL GOWN PRINCIPLE

Any time I begin to grow weary in hospital church ministry, it seems that the Lord brings along another e-mail, letter, or phone call that reminds me of the importance of what we're doing. I regain my perspective and am reminded why hospital church style ministries are so important.

A few years ago, I received an e-mail from a woman I'll call Debbie. About ten years ago she and her family attended Celebration Fellowship for nearly a year and then moved to a different state. In the e-mail Debbie recounted how, on a recent Sunday morning, she had been home with a cold and unable to attend her current church, so she downloaded a message from our Web site. It brought back a number of memories for her, so she wrote, "I felt that you should know the impact that you as a church had on our lives." Her story is best heard in her own words:

> We first learned of Celebration through our neighbors. Little did we know how crucial that connection would become to our marriage and family. At the time we were involved in

another church. We were the "darlings" of that church, and everyone thought we were on top of the world. But no one knew the pain that was in our marriage and how much we were hurting. Then our lives fell apart. We went from being leaders in our church to the latest subject of juicy gossip. You see, my husband had been having an affair with a woman in the church and was exposed. He fell hard and far, and his fall took me and our kids with him. All of a sudden we were taboo in the church, and no one knew quite what to do with us.

Thankfully, six months earlier we had visited Celebration on a whim. We had just wanted to check out what our friends were so excited about. During your message that day you had said, "Celebration will always be a church where the hurting can come. No one will be turned away because of past mistakes." In other words, it was a place where the broken could be restored. At the time of that first visit I had no idea that my husband was having an affair, so I had no idea how important that visit would become for our lives. However, your words stuck with us. When we could no longer attend our church because of embarrassment and others' hatred for my husband, we came back to Celebration.

You accepted us and prayed for us. Your church led us through a process of beginning again and restoration in our marriage. There was never a time that Celebration made us feel uncomfortable or unworthy of being there. You simply accepted us where we were and loved us through a very difficult time. After nine months of being at Celebration, my husband's job led us to another state where we lived for one and a half years. While we were there we were able to separate ourselves further from everything that had happened and bond again as a couple and a family. It was God's perfect timing for us.

We have now been back in Texas for the past several years, in another city, and we are serving in places of leadership in our church. We are both on the praise team and have the joy of leading others in worship. It is such a blessing to have come full circle and have the restoration that only God could provide.

I tell you this to let you know that what you and Celebration do every week really does make a difference in people's lives. I am so thankful for the support and love you gave us during the time we were there. You are reaching people that other churches don't want to deal with, and tackling problems that churches don't want to admit even exist. Celebration was the "Jesus" we so desperately needed to see. I, my husband, and my children will forever be grateful to you and your ministry. Thank you so much for caring for our broken family, and being an instrument of restoration. May God continue to bless and use you all.

## A SAFE PLACE

When people are hurting, when they are broken and poured out, they need a safe place. After hearing hundreds of stories similar to Debbie's (and many that are much worse), we have discovered that people often don't view church as a safe place. This is not only true of those who are outside of the church, but even many Christians don't see their local church as a safe place. When life happens and the bottom falls out, people go outside of their local church for help. It should not be so. That is so contrary to how Jesus, who is the head of the body, saw Himself and the church that He came to establish.

In Mark 2:14–17, Jesus was attacked by the Pharisees, the religious elite of His day, for associating with the outcasts and the hurting. Jesus responded in verse 17: "It is not those who are healthy who need a physician, but those who are sick; I did not come to call the righteous, but sinners." The Pharisees were righteous only in their own eyes, not in the eyes of God. Jesus chided them for their hypocrisy on several occasions. Their main focus was on outward appearances, and making those look good. But Jesus said that inside they were full of dead men's bones (Matt. 23:27).

I know several medical doctors who are a part of the Hospital Church. If they were willing to treat only those who were not sick, they would soon go out of business. Doctors go to medical school to learn how to treat sick people! This simple concept may well be one of the keys to what is wrong with the church in America. Many, it seems, want to minister to those who are well. The hurting stuff is just too messy. Yet Jesus gravitated toward those who were hurting, and they gravitated to Him. If the church isn't a safe place, then people either won't get help or will go outside the church of Jesus Christ for the help they need. Either one is an indictment on the church as it exists today in America.

Why is it that the typical local church in America is seen by so many as an unsafe place? Perhaps we have been guilty of rewriting the gospel in the church in America. The rewrite goes something like this: *If you just love Jesus enough, then you won't struggle in your life.*

According to this false gospel, love for Jesus is the only criterion to wholeness. Christians with an extreme love for God don't struggle in their marriages, don't get depressed, don't have anxiety in their lives, and most certainly don't experience moral failure. Just loving Jesus is the answer.

Granted, in most places that message isn't put out on a billboard or in the church bulletin, but it is the unspoken subtext to virtually everything that goes on. Are any of the following subtexts evident in your church?

- We're expected to put on our happiest faces whenever we come to church.

- There's pressure for every family to look like it's in order.

- Every church service must end with a joyful, upbeat song, because we want people to leave happy. We would never end with a somber song, or even with a contemplative one, or certainly not a song of confession. It's just not what people want these days when they leave a church service. We want people to leave smiling. That way they'll come back.

- We don't talk a lot about sin in our church—sin is too depressing.

- We pronounce people "well" or "healed" in prayer. Healing is an instant event. If people are still hurting after that, it's indicative of a lack of faith on their behalf.

- We are careful about our prayer requests, lest we reveal too much of the real us.

- There are some things we could talk about in our small groups, but there are definitely other things we couldn't talk about. It just wouldn't be right.

- If someone's in pain in our church, there's not much we can do for him except refer him to counseling.

- We preach sermons about victory in Jesus but seldom go on to explain what the New Testament really says about how victory happens—except just to love Jesus more.

- We sort of need to be guarded about what we say and do at our church. It's best to think through something before you say it, unless you want to get criticized later on.

- If someone who attends our church overtly sins (i.e., has an affair or something) it's probably a good thing for that person if they stop coming or go to a different church.

- The unspoken rule in our church is protection—we want our church to be a place where respectable families can come and worship the Lord.

In these atmospheres we don't dare reveal the truth about the things going on in our lives, because other people will think that we don't love Jesus enough! We all want others to think we love Jesus. So we suffer or struggle in silence until disaster strikes. Then we just fade away. When we go, people say things like, "Oh, that's too bad. I thought they really loved Jesus. I guess not."

By this false gospel standard, the average bar is a safer and more honest place than the typical North American church. At least at the bar people can tell their troubles to each other, even if there is no help to be found there.

I can promise you that I have loved Jesus since the day that He saved me from a sure and certain life of hell on earth like my father's, and from a literal hell in eternity. But that didn't stop my life from eventually beginning to crater, even though I was a pastor. I loved Jesus till I was blue in the face. But that didn't negate the fact that I had emotional wounds in my heart that I had never addressed or found healing for. I loved Jesus, but that didn't make the pain go away. In many ways it made the pain worse, because all the things I had at one time used to self-medicate were no longer options. I was left clueless about what to do with my pain. I thought I just needed to find a way to love Jesus more and it would go away! All along, the Jesus that I loved, the great physician, wanted to bring healing in my heart. But I didn't have a safe place to heal. I didn't have a hospital for Him to do His healing work. I didn't even know what work needed to be done.

This reality is brought home to me on almost a weekly basis. With increasing regularity we have families who come to our Hospital Church to find help either because their church wasn't a safe place to seek it or because their church didn't have a clue how to help them. Very often their problem seems to revolve around the problem of addiction. We live in the most addicted culture in human history, and it isn't getting better (I'll say more about this in chapter 10). We are always willing to help those who seek it, even if they don't regularly attend Celebration. But every time other churches refer people to us it breaks my heart, simply because hurting people should be able to find the help they need right there in their own church family! We have had staff members of other churches come to our freedom groups, because they knew they would lose their job if they got honest at their church. Someone once said, "The Christian army is the only army in the world that shoots its wounded." This should not be so.

Just recently it happened again. I got a call from a desperate mom and dad. Their thirty-five-year-old son is addicted to alcohol, drugs, sex, and who knows what else. He is currently living out of his car in a seedy part of town. These are wonderful Christian people. They have a daughter with a Ph.D. who does mission work around the world. They are active in their faith and in their church. Their heart is breaking for their son, and they don't know what to do.

They came in to my office and told their story. They had gone to their pastor and their church, and neither had anything to offer them other than, "We will pray for you." Prayer is crucial—no doubt about that—yet this situation requires physical help and action. We must put feet to our prayers. I spoke to them about issues such as how the addictive cycle works and about the danger of enabling. Then I suggested that they come to Celebration on Sunday morning. Not to proselytize them, but so they could get a chance to meet people who once were where their son currently is, so they could see that there is hope.

Wonderfully, they said that their son might come with them. He did. On Sunday morning, after spending the night in his car, he went to their house, took a shower, and came to church with them. As they stood there just inside the door to the auditorium, I began bringing people over to them and making introductions—people who were once living in slavery to addictions, pain, and destructive behaviors but are today living in victory and healing. What was amazing was that there were so many. Everywhere I looked there was someone I could tap on the shoulder to come and meet these people and their son. Person after person told their story. These were people from all walks of life: professionals, business owners, flight attendants, truck drivers, all walks of life. I looked their son in the eye and said, "There is hope, and there is help. But we can't do it for you. We can't push a rope. You have to want help, and when you do, we are here."

Another family came to us three years ago, from a large, well-known church in our city. This family had a twenty-something son who was an alcoholic. They too are wonderful Christian people, active in their faith, with daughters that love the Lord (at one time they were missionaries in Mexico). But their son was bent on self-destruction, and their church had nothing to offer them. Their son got help and is in recovery. Three years later they are helping another family like them find help. Today, that father is serving as an elder in our church.

We as Christian leaders must create safe places if people are going to get honest and be healed. What does that safe place look like? Let me share three key components with you. I'll share them within the context of what we did at Celebration Fellowship, not as a description of a step-by-step plan you must do, but as principles that worked for us. Each body of believers should hammer out the specifics within the individual needs of their own ministry environments.

## VITAL COMPONENTS OF A HOSPITAL MINISTRY

The Hospital Church goal is to provide a safe place that helps facilitate life transformation. Several years ago, I heard Erwin McManus teach about making whole disciples out of broken people. He used three terms that I've borrowed here, although our application of these terms in the Hospital Church is different from the way he used them. Consider these terms the three vital components for creating a church of safety:

### #1: Integrity

Integrity is an integral part of life transformation, emotional healing, and growth. We are living with integrity when the image we project on the outside is a true picture of what is actually going on inside. Integrity is when we stop hiding.

Jesus' harshest words were directed at those who lived without this type of integrity (see Matt. 23). On the outside these hypocrites presented a pristine picture. On the inside, Jesus said, they were "full of dead men's bones" (Matt. 23:27). Integrity is God's intention. It's part of His design for the world. You'll never peal an apple and find a banana inside.

The problem of a lack of integrity began in the garden of Eden. Before Adam and Eve sinned they were naked and just fine with that (Gen. 2:25). Who wouldn't be? But when sin entered the equation, they covered up (3:7). We have been covering up ever since. Adam and Eve used leaves. We use all kinds of things—education, money, success, and yes, even religious behavior—to cover up the truth of what is really going on inside.

For emotional healing to take place, we must come to the place of integrity. We have to be willing to tell our secrets to trusted people in trusted environments! That is why brokenness is often necessary before people will begin the healing process. In brokenness there are no secrets because there's no more reason to hide. At the place of brokenness the most important thing in the world is simply to get well!

The Bible says that we are to confess our sins to God. 1 John 1:9 says, "If we confess our sins, He is faithful and just to forgive us our sins and to cleanse us from all unrighteousness" (NKJV). But that isn't the end of the story. James 5:16 says, "Confess your sins to one another, and pray for one another so that you may be healed." The immediate context of that verse may be about physical healing, but the principle applies to every kind of healing. What we keep hidden inside is what keeps us from getting well.

Around the Hospital Church we have a saying: "Secrets put bullets in the Enemy's gun to shoot you with." The Enemy uses our secrets to destroy us. When we keep secrets, we load his pistol with ammunition; then he shoots us with it. Another way of saying this is that "we are only as sick as our secrets." Secrets create fear, shame, and despair. When I don't have any secrets from you, I don't have to live in fear that you are going to discover something about me that I don't want you to know. Disclosure sets me free from fear! But people need a safe place to tell their secrets.

Recently a couple began attending the Hospital Church. The husband started coming to our Saturday morning men's group, where about fifty men gather at 8:00 AM for freedom groups. The first morning he came we talked about transparency, integrity, and the need to do away with our secrets. It was the third morning that he was in the group that he spoke up and delivered a powerful statement:

"I was in prison for ten years. Since I have been out I have been fearful of letting people know about my past. But this morning, listening to all of you men tell your stories openly and without shame, I realized that what I have done is trade one prison for another. I spent ten years in a prison with bars, and since then I have lived in a prison of fear—a fear of what people would think of me, how they would act toward me if they knew. I don't want to live in that prison of fear anymore. I need to tell you who I am, what I have done, and where I have been."

That morning he began to be set free for good.

One of the most moving experiences I have ever had in ministry came in the mid-1990s. It illustrates the power of a safe place. Two single adults came into our church. They didn't know each other initially. Laurie was a single mother and an alcoholic. She got into recovery through AA and then came to Christ at the Hospital Church. Mario had recently been divorced and carried a lot of pain from his past. They both got into our freedom group process and began to experience emotional healing and spiritual growth. Eventually Laurie moved into leadership as a facilitator in freedom groups. Mario began to facilitate a divorce recovery group. They met and started dating. They made a commitment to sexual purity in their relationship and set up boundaries to help facilitate that commitment. One of those boundaries was that when Laurie's children went to bed, Mario went home for the evening.

One night they didn't observe their boundary, and they blew it morally. They discussed it with each other, confessed it to God, and received His forgiveness. Weeks later they found out that Laurie was pregnant. They immediately went to their lay pastor (community group leader) and told him about what had happened and about the pregnancy. He told them that they needed to speak with me about it, since they were both in leadership in the church. They came in and told me everything. I told them that everything they had done to this point was right (except the sex outside of marriage part, obviously)—they had confessed their sin to God and had reestablished their boundary. They had gone to the right people and openly confessed. Therefore, the issue at hand wasn't church discipline. (That is for when a Christian is unrepentant.) The issue we had to deal with was how they could be restored in the body of Christ without fear or shame. I told them the only way that could happen was by full disclosure. They could go ahead and get married and hope that people couldn't do the math (you know, nine months and all). But people aren't stupid, and neither were Mario and Laurie. They would always live in fear that someone was going to put the numbers together and figure out what they had done. The secret would harm them, and we needed to take the bullets out of the Enemy's gun.

They were willing to disclose their sin to the entire church body, and they would have been able to do that at our church in a safe environment. However, I felt that it would be better for them to disclose to the leadership only, since we had a monthly leader's forum that would be more conducive to that. They agreed.

With tears, they stood before the leaders in our church, confessed their failure, and asked for forgiveness as they had asked for God's forgiveness. Then one of the most incredible things I have ever witnessed happened. Without prompting, en masse, that group of leaders (about 75) got up from their seats and began moving toward the stage where Mario and Laurie stood. Mario and Laurie then knelt on the stage and those leaders gathered around them, laid their hands on them, and prayed for them for the next ten minutes. They prayed prayers of love and support. They prayed prayers of encouragement. They prayed prayers of God's blessing on this couple who had just confessed their sin openly! There wasn't a dry eye in the house.

When Mario and Laurie stood up from that experience, they were set free from fear, shame, guilt, and despair. The Enemy's gun was empty. He had no ammunition to shoot them with. There were no secrets! That next Sunday when they came to church, they didn't have to slink down the halls, hang their heads, or sit on the back row. Soon they got married. Eventually they moved away to another state, because of a work-related transfer, but they still come back and visit the Hospital Church when they can. They always walk in with their heads held high.

It takes a safe place to accomplish a miracle like that. The first component of creating this kind of safe place is integrity. We must get honest to be healed.

## #2: *Perseverance*

As has already been stated, change is a process not an event. Emotional healing takes time, sometimes a long time. Healing is often painful, too. If you don't go through the surgery you don't get the healing. To experience long term change and real healing requires perseverance.

Sometimes we see people begin the healing process and quit. After a few weeks of looking into those bags of emotional garbage, it's just too painful for them to deal with. We always encourage them to begin again the next time a new group starts up. We have had people begin a freedom group for healing three or four times before they are willing to press through and go the distance. In twelve-step circles they sometimes refer to this as "the recovery three-step." Sometimes someone will begin the program, do steps one, two, and three, but when they come to step four, taking "a searching and fearless moral inventory" it is too much for them and they quit. That's too much honesty, pain, and introspection, so they quit.

Healing comes through perseverance in the process. A dear friend, with whom I meet regularly for honest reflection and accountability, was a practicing alcoholic for forty years before he got sober and came to Christ. When people ask him how he became an alcoholic he says with a grin, "Practice, practice, practice." When people ask him how he healed after so many years of destructive behavior he says the same thing, "Practice, practice, practice." That's perseverance: doing the right things over and over because they are the right things to do.

We have discovered that people will persevere only if they have a safe place to move at a pace they can manage. If people are not ready to stay with the process the first time they begin, we must to be willing to allow them to make that decision. We can encourage, we can pray, we can support, but we can't do it for them. Part of being a safe place is being able to say to them, "We will be here for you when you are ready!"

All around Celebration Fellowship we have banners that direct people to various places. On the bottom of each of those banners are three words. Help, Hope, Healing.

Help, Hope, Healing.
Help, Hope, Healing.
Help, Hope, Healing.

Those words now are on just about everything we print, because those words communicate three elements of a safe place. Let's take a closer look at each of those words within the context of perseverance:

### Help

We all need help. No one ever does much in this life that amounts to anything by going it alone. The work of the Hospital Church is all done in community. It is about people helping people in Christ's name, by Christ's strength, and according to the truths of His Word.

The hospital church ministry is not driven by the professional staff. It is driven by people who have been helped and now give of themselves to help others in Christ's name. When someone comes out in the open about his pain or struggle, the first thing I tell him is, "I have some people I want to get you connected with." That is because I know that if he is ever going to be able to persevere on the difficult journey ahead, he is going to need help. I never cease to be amazed at the incredible generosity that is demonstrated by people in the healing process toward people who are hurting and needing help.

Paul said in 1 Thessalonians 2:8, "Having so fond an affection for you, we were well-pleased to impart to you not only the gospel of God but also our own lives. . . ." We all need help to persevere in the difficult process of healing. It doesn't depend upon me as the pastor. It is people-to-people ministry. People helping people.

### Hope

Hopelessness is a very dangerous thing. People give up when they lose hope. One of the ways people get hope, in the early stages of healing, is by keeping a proper perspective. In the Hospital Church, each person is at a different stage of the healing and growth process. We tell everyone not to focus on how far they have to go but on how far they have come! For most of us, if we focus on how far we have to go, we could lose hope. If we keep the focus on how far we have come, we gain hope.

Encouragement and affirmation gives people hope. I have told people for years these simple words of encouragement. "If you are in the process, the Father is pleased." God is pleased! In fact, when I say those words, tears often begin to flow in people's eyes. So many people have never believed that the Father could be pleased when He looks at them. They don't believe that they could achieve at a high enough level to please Him. They need to hear that pleasing the Father isn't about never failing. He doesn't demand perfection from His children, just progress. Only Jesus was perfect. But you and I never will be perfect until Jesus appears. As 1 John 3:2 says, "Beloved, now we are children of God, and it has not appeared as yet what we will be. We know that when He appears, we will be like Him, because we will see Him just as He is." Those are great words of hope. Someday, we will be like Him! In the meantime we can stay in the process, make progress, and be blessed in the knowledge that the Father is pleased.

People find hope through hearing the stories of healing in other people's lives. At the Hospital Church, we tell our stories of progress at every opportunity. We focus on how far we have come, not how far we have to go.

In Romans 5:5, Paul reminds us that "hope does not disappoint." People need hope to persevere through the process.

### Healing

In the early stages of the process, growth and healing will come in small increments and in little victories. It may be something as small as telling a freedom group a thing that has never been verbalized before. That is a victory over fear—telling a secret that has created fear and sickness. It is taking a bullet out of the Enemy's gun. That should be celebrated! Milestones, both big and small, are to be celebrated because they are indicators of progress and that healing is happening.

In twelve-step groups, they celebrate dates of sobriety. One month, a year, two years, five years, and on and on. One of my friends recently celebrated twenty years. These times of celebration are not meant to cause the person pride or complacency but to give encouragement and support for the growth and healing that has been experienced. It also gives a person encouragement for the growth that is ahead. Healing is a marathon, not a sprint. We would do well to cheer for each other along the way, rather than waiting until the finish line is crossed. Doing so will help us all to persevere in the race marked out for us.

We have a young man in our church in his upper twenties. He just celebrated six years of sobriety from alcohol. He was led to Christ by the police officer who had arrested him. The young man was on probation already and knew that the next stop for him was prison. The Christian officer saw his desperation and said, "You know there is a better way." The officer shared Christ with him, and the young man gave his life to Jesus. He was a clean slate back then, when it came to spiritual things, the Bible, church, the whole ball of wax. But he has persevered in all things; sobriety, the study of God's Word, emotional healing, and spiritual maturing.

This young man is doing so well today! For a time on Sunday morning he led a young singles' adult Bible fellowship in our church. One summer he went with us to youth camp as a camp counselor. Who'd have thunk it six years ago! I love to come up to him and put my arms around his big shoulders and say, "I am so proud of you. The Father is so proud of you. I really am, and He really is." He isn't perfect, and there is still much work to be done. He's had some setbacks along the way. We all have them, don't we? But I can't keep from rejoicing at the work that has already been done in his life. This young man is persevering through the process, but he isn't doing it alone. He has help, hope, and healing every step of the way to keep him going.

#### #3: Wholeness
Along with integrity and perseverance, the third vital component for creating a church of safety is wholeness. Wholeness is

the goal of the entire process, the motivation for having a church of safety. It is why we tell the secrets and do the hard work of biblical introspection. It's why we persevere when the process gets painful.

Wholeness is when the pendulum swings from receiving to giving. When someone begins the healing process, sometimes all they can do is receive. That's okay for a while. But over time, the goal of the process is for them to become less needy and begin to give as well as receive. Wholeness. Often in the Hospital Church, this is when people move into being a cofacilitator of a freedom group, and perhaps eventually a facilitator. Perhaps they become a mentor to someone newer in the process. Maybe they serve in some capacity completely unrelated to the freedom group process. The key is that they begin to give themselves away and begin to impart life to others. It's a powerful thing that happens when a church has been doing a hospital church ministry long enough that there is a large population of these people. These people radically change the spirit and the dynamic of the church.

What could possibly motivate these people to give their very own lives so sacrificially? There really is only one answer. Gratitude. Until a person comes to the place where she connects with the magnitude of what she has been given, she will continue to take. Gratitude moves people into wholeness—both gratitude to God and gratitude to God's people.

An interesting thing has happened at Celebration in the seventeen years since we transitioned into the hospital church ministry. Every year from 1992 to 2008 the church giving exceeded the budget. In fact, the budget grew more than 500 percent in those years. On top of that, we were debt-free until we completed a 30,000-square-foot children's facility in 2009. Even then, the debt we took on that building was only 25 percent of the construction cost. All of this in spite of the fact that I never preach about giving. In fact, I am very careful not to because that is one thing that hurting people are suspicious of the church about. They often think the church is interested only in getting their money. We don't do an annual budget campaign. We have never hired an outside stewardship campaign company to raise money for us. We are not a wealthy church. In fact, we are fairly average as per capita income goes.

So how did all of this happen? I have only one explanation. When people's lives are genuinely being transformed, they give out of gratitude not duty. They give not only of their financial resources, but of their time and their lives to others. It is just one more expression of wholeness.

We want to move people into integrity, so we walk them through perseverance and encourage them toward wholeness. That is how a safe church is created.

## THE PICTURE OF A SAFE PLACE

For years I have contemplated the design of the dreaded hospital gown. Who came up with this thing? Is it some leftover from medieval times? Is it someone's idea of a joke? I have never met anyone who liked the thing. It wasn't designed for making a fashion statement, that's for sure. Nor was it designed with the modest person in mind. The designer of the hospital gown had one goal. Easy access. The gown is designed to make getting to the nether regions of the body as easy for the caregivers as humanly possible.

It's interesting how for the first few days in a hospital a patient tries to hold on to at least a little bit of his dignity. He keeps the gown pulled down over his knees and is careful to keep the flaps in the back overlapping. But then, after a few days in the hospital, after being poked and prodded over every part of his body, that caution goes away. You see a guy walking down the hall with the back wide open and flapping in the breeze. By this time, everyone in the place has already seen everything he's got. Why hide anything?

People don't go to a hospital for vacation. People check into the hospital because they recognize something is wrong and they need help. Everyone is there for the same reason—help, hope, and healing. What a picture of what the church should be: a place where all of us can come together, put on our hospital gowns with the back flaps open—without fear, shame, or inhibition—and heal together. Philip Yancey writes in *The Jesus I Never Knew*:

The more unsavory the characters, the more at ease they seemed to feel around Jesus. People like these found Jesus appealing: a Samaritan social outcast, a military officer of the tyrant Herod, a quisling tax collector, a recent hostess of seven demons. In contrast, Jesus got a chilly response from more respectable types. Pious Pharisees thought him uncouth and worldly, a rich young ruler walked away shaking his head, and even the open-minded Nicodemus sought a meeting under the cover of darkness. . . .

How strange this pattern seemed, since the Christian church now attracts respectable types who closely resemble the people most suspicious of Jesus on earth. What has happened to reverse the pattern of Jesus' day? Why don't sinners like being around us?

Somehow we have created a community of respectability in the church. . . . The down-and-out, who flocked to Jesus when he lived on earth, no longer feel welcome.[1]

In essence, the observation that Yancey is making here is that we, the American church, have the reverse effect on people that Jesus had. The people who were comfortable with Jesus are uncomfortable with the church today. The people who were uncomfortable with Jesus are comfortable with the church today. The church has become a safe place to those who felt unsafe with Jesus. And we have become unsafe to the very ones who felt safe with Jesus, and with whom He spent most of His time.

What made hurting people gravitate toward Jesus? I think one of the reasons is that Jesus dealt honestly and openly with the real issues of life. Perhaps that's what made Him unsafe to those who refused to recognize their need, but it made Him incredibly safe and attractive to those who knew they were eaten up with need. I think Jesus intended for all of us to put on our hospital gowns . . . and leave the back untied.

1. Philip Yancey, *The Jesus I Never Knew* (Grand Rapids: Zondervan, 2002), 147–48.

## THE PROCESS OF BUILDING A SAFE PLACE

The church today that desires to be like Jesus by being a safe place for hurting people must continue asking the question: What made hurting people gravitate toward Jesus? And as you discover the answers, you make adjustments.

Here is how the Hospital Church has built—and continually builds—a safe place for hurting people. Again, I present these as generalized principles and invite you to make the specific applications to your own church within the context of who you are, not who we are.

### #1: Find the balance between legalism and license

Legalism means living life completely by rules. License means having no rules at all. Those are the two extremes that people in Jesus' day moved toward, and they are still the extremes that churches today move toward. But Jesus stood in a balanced place between the two. This doesn't mean He took a little bit of legalism and a little bit of license, put them together, and found a middle ground. What it means is that Jesus knew of a place that is between those two, and that is where He lived His life. That place is called grace.

John 8:1–11 describes how the scribes and the Pharisees brought a woman who had been caught in the act of adultery and threw her in front of Jesus. "In the Law Moses commanded us to stone such women," they said. "What then do You say?"

John tells us that they were doing this to test Jesus. This was the dilemma: If Jesus said, "Let her go," they could condemn Him as a lawbreaker and a heretic and could be done with Him. If He said, "Stone her," then Christ's followers would have deserted Him. They certainly wouldn't want to hang around with Him if He was going to side with the legalists. Jesus' movement would fall apart, and the Pharisees wouldn't have to bother with it anymore.

Christ shocked them by demonstrating neither legalism nor license but grace. He knelt down and began to doodle in the sand. We don't know exactly what He wrote, but then He stood up and said, "He who is without sin among you, let him be the first to throw a stone at her."

Over the next few moments the legalists, one by one, dropped their stones and walked away. When it was just Jesus and the woman He asked, "Woman, where are they? Did no one condemn you?" She replied, "No one, Lord." And Jesus said, "I do not condemn you, either. Go. From now on sin no more."

Jesus didn't condone her sin. He confronted her destructive behavior while at the same time offering her hope. That is what grace does. Grace doesn't wink at sin. It also doesn't throw stones. Grace challenges sinners to change, to grow, to get better, and it refuses to give up on someone.

In the Christian community, real grace is hard to find. We tend to gather around the two poles; law or license. As a pastor, I have pondered this problem for many years. I have to confess to you that for years my personal tendency was to move toward the pole of law. I knew that was wrong, and I fought it with everything that was in me. I think I struggled for so long with the lure of that extreme simply because the other extreme of license was so distasteful to me. I had already lived at that pole before I came to Christ, and I was darned sure I wasn't going to go there again. So, because I wasn't mature enough to understand true grace, I kept being repelled by license and drawn toward law. I have agonized over this dilemma, and in that agony some things have become clear to me. Let me contrast these three positions for you as it has come to me:

Legalism is self-righteousness.
License is self-destruction.
Grace is self-denial.

Grace is at the same time the most liberating and most difficult place to live. Grace means that I have to completely depend upon God, not only for my salvation but for every decision of every day. That is difficult to do, and it makes us incredibly uncomfortable.

We struggle with grace because we want to be in control. Although law and license are opposites, they arrive at the same result. They give me control. I like control. Grace is the only place where I lose all control. That's uncomfortable, and in my human nature I don't like it. In both legalism and license it's all pretty much cut-and-dried—either do what my rule book tells me to do, or do what my flesh tells me. Both are clear and easy. Grace requires that we remain sensitive in every situation, in every event of life, to hear from the Spirit of God for direction. Grace is messy. Grace is difficult. Grace is uncomfortable.

For most of us who are sincere Christians, legalism seeks to honor God (that's what we tell ourselves). But it always fails and ends up dishonoring God. Even the Pharisees, the legalists of their day, in the beginning had motives to honor God. The Pharisaical movement was born at a time in the life of Israel when God's people had virtually lost their connection to the portion of the Word of God they had, the Old Testament. The Pharisaical movement was born as a call to God's people to come back to His Word. That was a good thing. But it degenerated over time into a rigid, unbending, judgmental system of legalism that went far beyond the Word of God. They took the Ten Commandments, which are a perfect reflection of the moral nature of God, and before they were done with them they had 248 commands, and 365 prohibitions. To these they tacked on 39 categories of activities that could not be performed on the Sabbath, and under each of those categories there were subcategories. All this, just about the fourth commandment.[2] With time, they began to honor their rules, commands, prohibitions, explanations, and exceptions more than the Ten Commandments themselves. That is what legalism always does. It perverts God's truth and character.

On the other hand, license, as it appears among some Christians, ostensibly seeks to honor the person—personal freedom, respect for the individual, and things like that. But, like legalism, it also fails to achieve its aim and ends up dishonoring the person. License degrades people. It reduces them to the level of animals who live by the dictates of the their basest desires.

2. Gerhard Kittel and Gerhard Friedrich, eds., *Theological Dictionary of the New Testament*, vol. 7, trans. Geoffrey W. Bromiley (Grand Rapids: Eerdmans, 1971), 14.

In contrast, grace honors both God and the person. Grace seeks to honor God with a moral and pure lifestyle and respect for His Word but deals with the reality of human failure with hope, forgiveness, and restoration, not stones. That is what Jesus did with the woman caught in adultery. Jesus didn't dishonor God or the woman by saying that what she had done didn't matter or was acceptable. Neither did He dishonor her as a creation of God by saying, "It's over for you! Stone her!" It would have been easier to either stone her or ignore her. But grace refused either extreme.

Legalism ignites fear.
License ignites the flesh.
Grace ignites faith.

When we live by law, we live in constant fear that we are going to mess up so bad that it's over for us. License just turns the beast of the flesh loose where it can run rampant and destroy everything in its path. Grace brings us to the place where we have to walk in a trust relationship with God for our every need, every insight, and all wisdom for every decision and eventuality of life. The testimony of Scripture is that neither fear (2 Tim. 1:7) nor the flesh (Rom. 7:14–25) honors God. Only faith does that (Heb. 11:6). In legalism there is no decision to make because there is a rule for every decision. In license there are no decisions to make at all. Just do whatever pleases you at the moment. In grace there are lots of decisions, and we must depend wholly on God for each one. That's tough. That's uncomfortable for beings whose fallen nature cries out for control.

A hospital church ministry has to function in grace. There is no alternative. Decisions have to be made about how situations will be handled that require grace. Many people who walk in the door of a church have already been wounded by an environment of law or by their own life of license. Grace is the only alternative for a safe place to heal. Mario and Laurie's story, already told in this chapter, required grace. Either law or license would have dishonored both God and them. Only grace would suffice in that situation. Their moral failure was not ignored. Neither were they condemned. Grace ruled the day. God was honored. Mario and Laurie were honored. The ministry was honored. The church was honored. That's what grace does. It brings honor to all involved.

The grace that Jesus showed was a key reason that the legalists were uncomfortable with Him. But it was also the key reason the outcasts and the hurting were drawn to Him. If the hurting are going to be attracted to the church today, the church must begin to model and live by that kind of grace. It's the key ingredient to creating a safe place for healing.

How do you create an environment of safety for the hurting? The desire to see your church develop into such a place is the most important thing of all. You have to teach it, sure, but you also have to want it.

### #2: Model transparency from the top down

The importance of the leadership in creating a safe place cannot be overemphasized. No matter what else is done in the church, if the pastor is not genuine, transparent, and honest about his own process of growth, no one will really believe the church is a safe place.

I recognize that there is debate about how much of his personal pilgrimage a pastor should share publicly. It's a valid debate, and I do accept that the pastor can go overboard in talking about his own struggles and process. When that happens, it can look and sound as if the preaching event is just a place for him to process his own life. People can get tired of hearing it. Or get grossed out or overwhelmed by it. However, on the other side, if he never shares from his vulnerability, people will become suspicious of whether he is for real, or if he has any clue about what real people are going through in their lives. He establishes the image of got it all together. It's a tough balance to strike. But if there has to be an error made, err on the side of transparency and openness.

Though Jesus was fully God, He was also fully human. His birth was nothing spectacular, just a stable, surrounded by the sounds and smell of animals. His childhood in His father's carpenter shop was about as ordinary as it comes. When He began His three-year public ministry He didn't set up shop in a posh office building, complete with fax machine and secretary. He was an itinerant who spent much of His time out under the stars. He wasn't embarrassed to show His emotions, from anger at those who were degrading the temple, to weeping over Jerusalem, or expressing frustration toward the disciples who just weren't getting it. All of this went to clearly establish His very down-to-earth humanness. That made Him both accessible and real to regular people.

In our fast-paced lives of modern ministry, with the growing crowds of expanding ministries, pastors have to fight the pedestal complex. People do tend to put pastors there, and it is a very dangerous place to live. We have to communicate that we are men just like they are, and that at times we have feet of clay just as they do. The preaching event is one place where this transparency can happen. Sharing our stories genuinely reminds people that we are real, and gives them encouragement in their own pilgrimage. We must show that we are in process as well.

Every time I stop in the midst of a message to share my personal experience of struggle, growth, and even failure, the atmosphere of the place suddenly changes. On a recent Sunday morning, because it was appropriate to the text and the message, I shared my struggle with the "poor white trash" recording in my head. I shared the reality of it, where it came from, and how I am daily learning to be "renewed in my mind" to overcome it. It was real, not contrived; it was sincere, not manipulative; it was from the heart, not just an illustration.

The response from people was overwhelming. They told me how it encouraged them in their own growth and healing to overcome the recordings that play in their head. There were probably people who two weeks later would not have been able to tell you what text I was preaching from, but they are still able to tell that story almost word for word. That's why I told it— because I have learned the impact that it has on people's lives when I share from my own experience. They don't lose respect for me as a pastor or as a leader. I gain their respect as a fellow pilgrim who can relate to their lives. And it communicates a safe environment for them.

For people to believe that the church is a safe place where they can heal and grow, they have to know that it is a place that is safe for everyone to heal, from the top down. We can tell them it is safe, but they won't really believe it until we prove it to them by taking the risk of our own vulnerability.

### #3: *Let people live their stories and then tell their stories*

One of the most gratifying things about doing Hospital Ministry is hearing the amazing stories of healing, life transformation, and growth that people have to tell. As long as I have been doing this work, I still never cease to be amazed by, nor do I ever grow tired of, hearing the stories. The impact those stories of life change can have on other's lives can't be overemphasized. When healing takes place in a person's life, others around them are touched and affected by that change.

On Christmas Eve 2005, a seventy-two-year-old man (I'll call him George) came to our church for the first time. In the New Year, he began to come on Sunday mornings. After a few weeks he called me up and asked for an appointment. As he sat down he announced right up front: "I don't believe in God, I don't trust people, I only trust animals."

"Well," I said, "I think we can work with that."

Over the next several months, about once a week George would come by to talk. He was a retired military man. He'd been in the Navy SeaBees, the construction arm of the Navy. His wife of many years had just passed away a few months before. Over the course of time I shared with him the way of salvation through faith in Christ. He listened and asked questions. We continued to meet and talk.

In mid-June he came in and sat down with an announcement that was as startling as the one that had begun our first visit. He said, "I want to be baptized this coming Sunday. This Sunday is my seventy-third birthday, and I think that would be a good day to be baptized."

"It would be a great day," I said, "but I have to ask you first about this commitment of your life to Christ thing. Have you made that decision?"

"I have," he said.

We talked some more and I was convinced that he had in fact trusted Christ as Savior. Then he said, "You know what brought me to this point? The change in the lives of my son and his wife. I have watched it happen, and that is what convinced me to begin coming to this church and make this decision."

Here's the story of what led up to George's decision: His son, Robert, who is in his forties, and his son's wife, Julie, had been coming to the Hospital Church for about a year. Julie had accepted Christ and begun to experience emotional healing from the wounds in her life through a loving freedom group. As she found growth and healing, she began to realize how unhealthy her marriage was. She separated from her husband for a while. Her husband, Robert, came to see me in turmoil over it all. We talked about his need for Christ and healing in his own life. He accepted Christ and began the change process. He started dealing with the issues in his own life. They eventually reunited in their marriage, and they have continued to grow and change.

The seventy-two-year-old dad was watching all of this, and it had a profound impact upon him. The trickle-down effect of the change in their lives was that a crusty old Navy man who had rejected Christ all his life gave his life to Christ and began his own spiritual journey. George passed away that same year he gave his life to Christ. His eternal destiny was changed through the testimony of change in his son and daughter-in-law.

That's the power of testimony. The one irrefutable evidence of the power of God to bring fragmented people into wholeness is the testimony of changed lives. So we celebrate the opportunity to first live that change, and then tell the story publicly. It's important that people have enough time to live it before they tell it. Others need to see the change before they hear about how the change happened!

We have two ways that we do testimonies at the Hospital Church. Sometimes, we will interview someone on camera, then edit that interview down to about a five-minute talk, put music in the background, and play it in our worship service. This is a powerful medium because it combines the emotional touch of music with the story. You have to be careful before you attempt this. Be sure that you have the equipment and personnel to do it in a reasonably professional way. Otherwise it can detract from the power of the testimony.

The other way we do it is to have people stand before the congregation and read their testimony. I always have people write it out word for word and then read it word for word. Most people who are not accustomed to speaking publicly are very nervous, and this helps calm them down. It also keeps people from chasing rabbits and getting distracted. When that happens, what really needs to be communicated gets lost. I never let someone get up and give his testimony extemporaneously for that reason. We keep the testimonies limited to five to seven minutes. That is long enough to tell the story but short enough that people's attention can be held.

The stories have to be told. They communicate that the church really is a safe place for healing.

### #4: Give priority in programming to hospital ministry

Some churches tack on a few groups to an already crowded weekly calendar and think they are getting it done. While that is better than nothing at all, it will never be very effective for two reasons.

First, people are already involved up to their ears. Although many of them need emotional healing at some level, they will never access it because they have only so many hours each week to give. The impact that emotional healing has on a person's family, work, and personal spiritual maturity make this process important enough to give it priority in the programming of the church.

Second, it communicates to people that the Hospital Ministry is not a priority. It says that this is just something that has been tacked on to everything else that is going on. When really hurting people come into the church, it subtly says that the church is not really a safe place. They will not feel like fully accepted and received members. They are just "those folks who are hurting," so we do a few groups to help them out. That may not be the attitude of the church (consciously at least) but that is the message that people will hear. It is a fact: we program according to priority.

At the Hospital Church, we meet as a large group only one time a week on Sunday mornings where we have two worship services and two fully graded Bible study hours. Everything else we do the rest of the week is small groups in homes and freedom groups that meet at the church. Wednesday nights are completely given over to freedom groups. The parking lot is full, and the classrooms are full of people in various kinds of freedom groups. We offer freedom groups on Thursday night as well. Recently we've begun to offer them on Saturday and Sunday mornings as well. We want to make them accessible to as many people as possible. What we are trying to say to people is that Hospital Ministry isn't something that we have tacked onto everything else. Hospital Ministry is a high enough priority that we give it priority in programming!

It isn't just what we do. It is who we are. It is a part of our DNA. When people come in and see all of the groups that are going on, and when they are meeting, they immediately say, "You people are really serious about this, aren't you?" Yes we are. We are deadly serious about it because it is a deadly serious issue and need.

## YOUR PLAN TODAY

I realize this has been a longer chapter, but it is one of the most important ones in the book. Churches must become safe places. There is no other solution. It is my prayer that this chapter has helped you see what steps you can begin to take in seeing your church become a place of safety.

What do churches of safety look like? Let me leave you with one illustration. Tony Campolo, in *The Kingdom of God Is a Party,* tells the story of a trip he made to Honolulu some years back. He suggests that some details about the setting have been changed, but you get the idea. Having crossed a few time zones, he found himself awake and wanting breakfast at about three o'clock in the morning by Hawaii time. He ended up in a greasy spoon in a sleazy part of town having coffee and a donut. While he was there, eight or nine prostitutes walked in after their evening's work. The place was small, so he soon found himself surrounded. He decided the best thing for him to do was to vacate the premises.

About that time, he overheard one of the prostitutes say, "Tomorrow is my birthday. I'll be thirty-nine." One of the others spoke up and said, "So? Whaddya want me to do about it? Bake you a cake?" The first one shot back, "Come on! Why do you have to be so mean? I'm just telling you about it. I don't expect anything. I've never had a birthday party in my life. Why should it be different now?"

Campolo hung around until they left and then asked the guy at the counter if those women came in every night. The guy said every night around 3:30 AM. Campolo asked if he could throw that prostitute a birthday party the next night. Her name was Agnes. The guy agreed. He said he'd even bake the cake. It would be an interesting break in the monotony of his life at least.

He must have gotten the word out because by 3:15 the next morning every prostitute who worked that area was in the little diner waiting. At 3:30, the prostitute named Agnes walked in. When she came through the door, Campolo jumped up and led the crowd in a yell of "Happy Birthday!" Agnes was so shocked that her mouth fell open, her legs nearly buckled, and someone had to grab her to steady her.

Then, as the cake was brought out, he led them as they all sang "Happy Birthday" to Agnes. Agnes was so overwhelmed she couldn't blow out the candles. She couldn't cut the cake. She just asked, "Is that cake mine?"

Campolo said, "It's all yours."

She said, "I can keep it?"

The cook said, "Go ahead and do what you want with it. It's your cake." Agnes picked up the cake, turned and walked out the door, carrying it as if it was a precious jewel.

The crowd was stunned into silence. Not knowing what else to do, Campolo said to the group, "What do you say we pray?"

He prayed for Agnes, for her salvation, and that God would touch her heart and change her life. When he finished, the cook turned to him and said with hostility, "You never told me you were a preacher. What kind of church do you belong to?!"

Campolo replied, "I'm from the kind of church that throws birthday parties for whores."[3]

That's a safe church.

---

3. Tony Campolo, *The Kingdom of God Is a Party* (Dallas: Word, 1990), 3–8

CHAPTER 9

# FORGIVENESS:
# THE SILVER BULLET PRINCIPLE

When I was a kid, I loved watching old horror movies. It always sent tingles down my spine to see the werewolf come out on a full moon and wreak havoc. The werewolf was in a class of monsters by himself: only one thing could ever stop him. You could shoot him with a bazooka, but that wouldn't do it. You could drive a stake through his heart like a vampire, but that wasn't it either. The only surefire way to do away with the werewolf was to shoot him with a silver bullet.

In modern times, the medical community has adopted the term *silver bullet* refer to a cure-all remedy for some physical ailment. Emotional healing can be a complex process, and there really isn't one cure-all remedy that causes it. However, one action comes so close and applies to so many people's lives, I consider it the silver bullet in emotional healing.

It's forgiveness.

Forgiveness is a core ingredient in the hospital church model of ministry. It's what much of the freedom group structure revolves around.. Forgiveness involves two components: we receive forgiveness from God for the wrong that we've done,

177

then we extend forgiveness to other people who have wronged us. Although both are important, my focus in this chapter is primarily the latter.

People need to forgive other people. This can be the greatest struggle people face. I've seen people go through decades of unnecessary pain because they haven't learned to forgive. Some go through their entire lives and never figure it out. When people don't learn to forgive, they get stuck in anger, hurt, disappointment, and frustration. The emotional results of unforgiveness can be devastating.

It has been our experience at Celebration Fellowship that when people learn to forgive, dams break and floodwaters of emotional healing rush in.

## THE CORE INGREDIENT

Why forgive?

It's like asking, why breathe? If a person doesn't forgive, death is imminent—maybe not physical death, but a type of slow spiritual and emotional death. A lack of forgiveness stifles and strangles a soul.

We need to forgive others because Jesus has forgiven us. In Matthew 18:21–35, Jesus told a parable about a certain king with a servant who owed him a huge sum of money. Out of kindness, the king forgave the debt. But then the forgiven servant refused to cancel the debt of another servant who owed him a far lesser amount. Word got back to the king about what had transpired between the two servants. The king called the first servant back in. "I forgave you freely and you should be willing to also freely forgive," he said, and threw the first servant into prison.

We need to forgive others because it's in our best interest to do so. Whenever I refuse to offer forgiveness it only causes *me* all kinds of grief. It allows the person who has already hurt me to continue to hurt me. The only way to stop the hurt is to forgive.

People mistakenly think that by withholding forgiveness they can somehow make the people who have wronged them pay for what they did wrong. But it doesn't work that way. When people don't forgive, it goes the other way: their own pain is compounded.

Hebrews 12:15 says, "See to it that no one comes short of the grace of God; that no root of bitterness springing up causes trouble, and by it many be defiled." Every time I refuse to forgive, a seed of bitterness is dropped into the soil of my spirit. I can choose to forgive my offender and crush that seed before it can take root, or I can choose not to forgive and watch that harmful seed grow into a toxic weed.

My unwillingness to forgive only causes me trouble. It contaminates and defiles my soul. The poison of this weed drains my joy and sickens my relationships. Over a prolonged period of time the stress of bitterness even has negative effects on my body. A lack of forgiveness sucks all the nutrients out of my life's soil, and nothing good can grow, emotionally, spiritually, or physically.

Forgiveness is possible! The Bible gives several powerful examples of people who were wronged but refused to allow bitterness to take root in their heart. Let's look at one recorded in Numbers 13–14.

God has delivered the Hebrew people out of slavery in Egypt, and they have come to the banks of the Jordan River. The Promised Land is within reach. Moses sends twelve spies into the land to check things out. But when the spies return, ten of the spies are filled with fear and insist that a conquest of the land is impossible. The people are swayed by the report and refuse to possess the land that God has promised. For their unbelief, God declares that they will wander in the wilderness until the entire faithless generation passes away. Only the two faithful spies, Joshua and Caleb, will live to enter the land. Only one problem: they have to wait forty years because of the unbelief of others.

Fast-forward in time. The faithless generation has all died, and Joshua has been appointed to lead them into the Promised Land. Caleb steps forward as a representative of the tribe of Judah and requests that Joshua give him the area of Hebron, the richest and most fertile in all the Promised Land. And Caleb receives it (Josh. 14)!

Here's the point: Caleb had been ready to receive the Promised Land forty-five years before he got to go in. Why the delay? Only because of the faithlessness of the rest of the nation! Caleb had to spend decades wandering in the wilderness because of other people's sin.

Imagine during that time in the wilderness how easy it would have been for Caleb to grow angry and bitter. When the days got long, the manna got monotonous, and sitting around the campfire every night got boring, how easy it would have been for him to focus on how they had cheated him out of what was rightfully his! But there is no indication in Scripture that he did that. As a result, he was able to enjoy his blessing.

Each one of us has a similar choice to make. Like Caleb, many of us have suffered in our lives due to the actions of others. Emotional pain is often the result of other people's unfair and harmful actions against us. But each of us must make a choice about what we are going to do with that pain. We can allow it to destroy us with bitterness. We can harbor anger and hatred and allow that to become toxic in our lives.

Or we can choose to forgive and be free.

## FORGIVENESS MYTHS

Misunderstanding about forgiveness can cause a great deal of damage and sometimes keep people from even attempting to forgive. These myths have to be dispelled from our minds before we can begin to understand what forgiveness really is and begin to really live it out. In the Hospital Church we are constantly reminding people of what real forgiveness is and is not. I want to point out three of the most damaging myths about forgiveness that we must dispel:

### Myth #1: If I forgive, that will minimize the wrong that was done

Sometimes forgiveness is withheld because we believe that if we forgive we are minimizing the wrong that was done to us. We mistakenly believe that forgiveness means writing off the enormity of whatever evil has taken place. Nothing could be further from the truth. To truly forgive we must first fully acknowledge the enormity of the wrong. If it wasn't a big deal to begin with, it wouldn't warrant forgiveness.

If someone has wronged you, then the hurt is real and the resulting consequences may have been devastating. Forgiveness doesn't mean that you have to minimize or deny the truth of that. Rather, fully acknowledge the pain and the hurt that it has caused you. Then quickly begin the process of forgiving.

In October 2006, an incredible tragedy took place in an Amish community in Pennsylvania. A man walked into a one-room schoolhouse and took several young girls hostage. He lined the girls up against a blackboard, then shot ten of them before turning the gun on himself. Six of the girls died; the rest were in serious condition.

The nation was astounded to hear the Amish community speak immediately about forgiveness. They directly offered forgiveness, not only to the deranged man who had terrorized and murdered their daughters but also to the man's shocked and grieving wife and family. Community members invited the man's wife to the funeral.

Forgiveness? Yes. But minimizing evil? No.

The Amish community's offer of forgiveness in no way minimized the horror of what happened. They were and are grieving deeply, as anyone would in their situation. But part of their healing is found in their forgiveness.

### Myth #2: Forgiveness means the relationship must be reconciled

Forgiveness and reconciliation are two separate issues. Sometimes both can happen; sometimes they can't. For reconciliation to happen, forgiveness is a must. However, reconciliation is not a must for forgiveness to happen. Reconciliation requires both parties to participate. Forgiveness requires only the participation of the one who was wronged.

Sometimes reconciliation is not possible. The person who wronged you might no longer be living. Perhaps his whereabouts are unknown, or she may not want anything to do with you. If reconciliation were a requirement for forgiveness, you could never forgive. Often, the other person is unwilling to admit the wrongdoing and ask for forgiveness. But you can still forgive. Forgiveness requires only your action.

In cases where a relationship cannot be reconciled, people have found an exercise called "the chair" to be helpful. There is nothing magical about it. It simply gives the person visible representation to work with. Here is how it works: You set a chair in front of you and imagine that the person you need to forgive is sitting in that chair. You speak to that imaginary person sitting in that chair as if the person were there. You visualize the person as you are expressing your forgiveness for what he or she did to you.

Sometimes we encourage people to write out exactly what they want to say and how they want to say it. You imagine that this is a letter that you are going to send to the person. When it is finished, the letter is never sent. It is the process of writing or verbalizing that is the healing part of either of these exercises. The point is that even when reconciliation is not possible, forgiveness and healing can be experienced.

I can illustrate this truth out of my life. For many years I never realized that I needed to forgive my father. I had denied that he had any effect on me. More than twenty years after his death, when there was no opportunity for any kind of reconciliation to happen, I realized how angry I had been at him for most of my life. I was angry primarily over a lost childhood and lost opportunities. After I accepted Christ and began to see the families of my Christian friends and my friends in college, for the first time I started to realize how far behind I was and what had already passed by in my life. That is when the anger began to manifest itself in me. The breaking point came after I was already a pastor.

Somebody asked me once to teach through the Ten Commandments on Sunday mornings. I said no, but then began to wonder why. Truthfully, every time I read the commandments I got stuck on one particular one: "Honor your father and your mother." How could I honor my father who had been so dishonorable?

I finally made the commitment to launch into the series and trust God that when I came to that commandment, He would give me something I could say. The week that I had to teach on the sixth commandment, God gave me something that I could honor my father for—God had used my father to give me biological life. It wasn't earth-shattering, but it was something to hold on to. There was nothing else about him that I could honor him for. But because I had been given biological life, I had the blessing of gaining spiritual life in knowing Christ. I also could experience the gift of my wonderful wife and children. Realizing the good things I enjoy because of the life my father gave me was the first step for me to be set free from my anger and forgive my father.

I shared the story of that revelation with the church as I taught on the sixth commandment. It was astounding how many people told me afterward how that word had given them hope to forgive their father or mother.

### Myth #3: If I forgive, I have to forget

Forgive and forget—it sounds so good on its face. But it seldom works that way. Try to forget something, and it will be all you think about. Some things are so hurtful and damaging, they are impossible to forget. It isn't the remembering that is the problem anyway. The problem is the power that memory has over you. The goal of forgiveness is not to have an event be released from memory. The goal is to be released from the power that memory has over you.

What forgiveness accomplishes is not forgetfulness but release. Forgiveness allows me to dig up the root of bitterness that has caused me so much trouble and has defiled my life and be set free from it. I still have the memory, yes, but the memory no longer has me. I am released from its power.

### FORGIVENESS FACTS

Once myths are dispelled, we can focus on what forgiveness is and how to accomplish it. The goal of a hospital church is to help hurting people understand that anyone can forgive anyone for anything—no matter how big. In fact, the greater the wrong, the more necessary forgiveness becomes. As the severity of the wrongs increase, so do the damaging effects of unforgiveness.

The greater the wrong, the more difficult it is to forgive, but also the more important forgiveness becomes. The need to forgive grows in proportion to the difficulty of the forgiveness.

In one of our freedom groups someone may say, "I could never forgive that person. What they did to me was so bad that I could never forgive." We will say, "The horrible nature of what they did to you makes it that much more imperative that you forgive."

Here are three truths about the nature of forgiveness. These truths show some of the nuts and bolts about how to forgive.

### Fact #1: Forgiveness is an act of the will

When the Bible speaks about forgiveness, it speaks about it as a command. Forgiveness isn't just a nice suggestion, it's a divine imperative. Jesus said, "Forgive, and you will be forgiven" (Luke 6:37 NIV).

Commands are directed at people's wills, not emotions. When someone is hurting it does no good to command, "Feel better!" Emotions can't be commanded. Forgiveness has to start as a decision, as an act of the will. We decide to forgive someone for something, because Jesus has told us to. Once we make that decision, emotions may or may not follow.

### Fact #2: Forgiveness means "to release"

In the Bible, the word that is translated *forgiveness* means literally "to release" or "send away." We still use the word this way sometimes when we speak of a debt. We forgive a debt. So when I forgive someone it means I am declaring: "You owe me nothing. There is nothing that I expect to get from you, so I release you." When I forgive a person I am releasing the person from my debt.

I saw on a recent TV program how the brother of Rachel Scott, one of the girls killed in the Columbine High School rampage of 1996, was practicing forgiveness. Craig Scott spoke about how his anger and rage had lasted for years after the shooting. After a while he realized he had to forgive his sister's killer, or else the anger inside him was eventually going to consume him. Craig shared the quote, "Forgiveness is like setting a prisoner free, and then finding out that the prisoner was you."[1] Wow! He spoke with such calm and peace that I knew for certain those were not just words. He had experienced that release personally.

What does it mean when we release someone who has wronged us? At Celebration Fellowship we tell people to picture themselves turning over the person to God. They are saying that if anything needs to be collected, they will leave it to God to collect it. God does a much better job of collecting whatever needs to be collected than you or I could ever do. Romans 12:19 says, "Never take your own revenge, beloved, but leave room for the wrath of God, for it is written, 'Vengeance is mine, I will repay,' says the Lord." If collection needs to be made, then it is God's job to do it.

### Fact #3: Forgiveness is an act of faith

If we are ever going to release the person who wronged us, then we have to trust in the character of God. We must trust that what He has told us about the need to forgive is true. We have to trust that He will deal with the person we release in a just way. It means that we must not only release the person to Him, but we must release control of the situation to Him.

What we have discovered in the Hospital Church is that before the issue of forgiveness can be addressed effectively, the subject of the character of God must be addressed. The first step of forgiveness is to clear up the confusion about the character and nature of God. He is just. He is faithful. He can be trusted!

A woman in our church named Joyce has experienced the release of forgiveness. Joyce is one of my heroes in the faith. Today she is the vice president of administration for a large international ministry. She's also helped begin a women's shelter that has partnered with our church. I asked Joyce if I could share her very personal experience of forgiveness. I will let her tell it in her own words as she wrote it:

---

1. *Dateline*, NBC, October 7, 2006.

In my recovery process there has been so much forgiveness I have had to do.

I've had to forgive the two men who took me at gunpoint, raped me, and left me in an area I was not familiar with. It took me over two hours to find my way to safety.

I've had to forgive my mother for not being there to protect me in my years as a little girl.

There were also other family issues and other people in my life who caused me much hurt and pain.

Forgiving myself was one of the hardest things I've ever done. I was very aware that some of my choices were hurting others as well as me, even at the time that I made them. I later felt great regret about that fact.

The release that had the most impact on me was forgiving my father. He was an alcoholic and was never there for me emotionally or physically in my growing up years. I remember wanting him to hold me, touch me, and talk to me, to say something other than yelling, "Get me another bottle of beer!"

You see, that was my job whenever he was home—to make sure there was never an empty bottle. Once in a while on a Saturday night he might be home if the television show "Last of the Mohicans" was on. It was his favorite. He would pass out in his chair after everyone else was in bed. I would make sure he was totally out, then climb up on his chair and put his arm around me. His arm was so heavy, but I would sit there with his arm over my shoulder and pretend he cared about me.

Later on I stopped caring if he cared about me and turned all of my hate and bitterness toward him. It spilled over into every relationship I ever had.

When he died at fifty-eight from cirrhosis of the liver, my statement to my family was, "I'm glad he is dead." I was severely scolded and pronounced the most despicable person around. I refused to go to his funeral service. Instead, I stayed in the funeral director's office, where he and I drank and had sex. Looking back, I think I was trying to get even with my dad, or just killing the pain in the way I had grown familiar with by that time.

After I started recovery, I realized I had to forgive him for not being the father I needed. It was difficult, but I did the "chair thing." I had come to understand that even if I didn't "feel" like forgiving, I could choose to forgive as an act of my will. I asked God to flow His forgiveness through me because I wasn't able to do it on my own. I had come to understand that I was a prisoner in a dungeon of bitterness and that a lot of the torture I endured was my own creation.

My unwillingness to forgive was holding me prisoner. I came to understand that I had the key to the cell. That key was forgiveness, and it was my choice to unlock the door and be free, or not. I had become comfortable in the cell, but at the same time I hated it. After a failed suicide attempt, I accepted that God was not going to allow me to die. If I had to live, I wanted to change my life.

What was amazing was that as I took the steps to forgiving my father it allowed me to grieve so many things. The loss of a father I never had. Loss of my self-worth. Loss of my children due to miscarriages. Loss of my marriages, and most of all, the loss of who God had created me to be. As long as I was focused on the wrongs others had committed toward me, my bitterness was allowed to deepen, and the walls of protection I had built grew higher and thicker. It took many years for them to come down. Sometimes it was a brick at a time. Sometimes an entire section would fall. It was all in direct proportion to how much I was willing to forgive others and forgive myself.

Sometimes I still grieve for the years I lost due to the bitterness and hate. Because of that, I want so much for others to know that forgiveness is the ONLY key that will unlock the self-made prison.[2]

Joyce's story illustrates so much the true nature of the forgiveness process. She needed to forgive without reconciliation, as her father was dead. She forgave as a decision of her will.

---

2. Joyce, personal correspondence to the author, 2005. Reprinted by permission.

And when she released her father, she was the one who was set free.

## HOW FORGIVENESS HAPPENS

In studying how Scripture applies to us today, it is helpful to see the difference between *descriptive* passages and *prescriptive* passages. Descriptive portions of Scripture describe how God worked in a certain situation, at a certain time, with a certain person or group of people. It does not necessarily mean He chooses to work that way all the time. For example, in Acts 5 the story of Ananias and Sapphira is told. They sold some land and pretended to give it all for the benefit of the early church while holding back some of the income secretly for themselves. God struck them down, and they died. That Scripture is descriptive in nature. It describes how God worked in that specific situation. It is not saying that is how He always works. Principles can be gleaned from this passage, but it can't be used as an illustration of how God always works.

Prescriptive portions of Scripture state a universal principle that applies to all people, in all situations, at all times. For instance, Galatians 6:7 states that whatever a man sows in his life, he will reap. That is always true. It may not happen immediately, or the way that we expect it to, but the kind of seed you plant will determine the harvest that comes in.

How does this apply to forgiveness? Scripture tells us we need to forgive. That is prescriptive, a command of God given for our own good. But there is no prescription about how we are to forgive, no formula in Scripture that prescribes a step-by-step process that must be followed. We can find principles in Scripture that help and guide us, but there is no formula given for forgiveness.

Forgiveness, like most things, is a process. Each person must negotiate this process for himself under the guidance of the Spirit of God. It may happen differently for you than it does for me. So, rather than give a formula for forgiveness, I want to mention three principles that we use in the Hospital Church to help people learn to forgive. I pray that these principles will help you to successfully negotiate the turbulent waters of forgiveness and help others to do the same.

### Principle #1: Seek to understand

You can never go wrong by seeking to understand the pain and hurt that another person has experienced. Someone has said, "We hurt others out of our own hurt." That is true. This doesn't excuse the hurt that we cause others or that others have caused us, but it does help us forgive . Remember, someone else is probably going to have to forgive you for hurt that you have caused him or her. Would you like for that person to attempt to understand what hurt and pain inside of you contributed to your hurtful behavior? Probably.

This was a step that helped me finally release my father. When I realized that I needed to forgive him, part of the process for me was to understand the pain that contributed to his senseless life.

My grandmother, who lived to be 103, was a controlling, vindictive, and selfish person. When I began the process of releasing my father from my debt, I went back and put myself in his situation. What must it have been like to be raised by my grandmother? I can't even imagine. What incredible emotional pain my father must have lived with his entire life. This didn't excuse anything he did in his life. He made his choices, and then those choices made him. But gaining perspective of the factors that informed his life helped me come to the place of forgiving him.

Seeking to understand is always a good thing.

### Principle #2: Always remember the forgiveness you have received

There is no forgiveness that I could ever be called upon to give to another person that could come near to matching the forgiveness I have received in Christ. When Jesus was hanging on the cross He prayed, "Father, forgive them; for they do not know what they are doing" (Luke 23:34). Jesus wasn't speaking only about those who physically nailed Him to the cross. He was speaking of me. I crucified Jesus. It was for my sin that He died. On the cross Jesus paid the debt of my sin that I might be forgiven by the Father freely, fully, and finally. He closed the book on the eternal penalty for my sin. What a great act of forgiveness.

About the time I begin to think something is just too much for me to forgive, all I have to do is go back to the cross. It helps me to keep it all in perspective.

### Principle #3: Focus on one person, one hurt at a time

Over the course of life some of us may have accumulated a long list of people who have wounded and hurt us. Because of this, the forgiveness process can look so massive that we may give up before even beginning.

Just this week the story came to me of a young man. It's so sad and horrible that it is difficult to even imagine. From ages four to fourteen, this man's father made him perform oral sex on him. Then an uncle raped him while his father watched.

How can forgiveness be possible with the enormity of this man's abuse? Without a doubt, if he is ever able to accomplish forgiveness, it will be a miracle of God. It also probably won't happen in a one-time event. The man will have to move through the forgiveness process one person, one act at a time.

When people come into the Hospital Church with a long list of hurtful experiences, we encourage them to look at the process one step at a time. How do you eat an elephant? One bite at a time. How do you forgive? One person, one act at a time.

## YOUR CHURCH'S SILVER BULLET

Forgiveness can happen. I've seen it over and over again. It often takes time. Often it happens in the strangest ways or in the people you would never imagine. But take heart. Forgiveness can become a core action in your local assembly.

When a woman named Cathy came to the Hospital Church a few years ago, she had very little life left in her. What she did have in her was a great deal of shame, bitterness, anger, and hate. Although on the outside there were issues such as alcoholism and promiscuity, the real problem was on the inside. Cathy had been a victim of sexual abuse, first from her grandfather and then from her first husband. The pain the abuse had caused in her, in her own words, "followed me day and night, relationship to relationship, and to the next drink or party."

The wounds from her first experience of abuse from her grandfather set her up to become involved with a man who would continue the abuse. When Cathy got pregnant, he began to beat her. He raped her, stole from her, and perpetrated his sexual addiction upon her. Her son died five days after he was born. Cathy eventually had to run away in the middle of the night to escape the abuse.

Deep inside Cathy realized that if she was ever going to have a life worth living, she would have to face the wounds of her abuse. In the Hospital Church, she became a part of a caring freedom group of other women who were also survivors of sexual abuse. In that group, Cathy found understanding and support. Over an eight-month process she began to experience the emotional healing that she so desperately wanted and needed.

Part of that process was facing the reality of what her bitterness toward her grandfather and abusive husband was doing to her. In the caring and supportive environment of her freedom group, Cathy began to learn the things about forgiveness that I have written here. She realized that she could forgive as an act of her will, without ever being reconciled to the abuser. By that time her grandfather was dead, and it was unsafe for her to reveal her whereabouts to her ex-husband.

Cathy began to forgive. She was determined not to allow her former abusers to rob any more of her life. For the first time in her life she experienced hope. Eventually, with the help of Christ and her freedom group of women, Cathy came to the pleasant realization that she had truly forgiven her former abusers. She had released them from her debt and into the hands of a just and caring heavenly Father.

Several years down the road, Cathy became a key part of the ministry of the Hospital Church to women who are survivors of sexual abuse. She, along with Joyce and other women, give their time and lives to help other women find freedom and healing in

Christ and in His body, the church. Is she still in the healing process? No doubt about it! But the more she gives away to others who are hurting, the deeper her experience of healing grows.

What a privilege to be a part of that. That's what a hospital church style ministry can do. Forgiveness is the core ingredient.

# PART FIVE

# The Big Issue

# CHAPTER 10

# THE COMING TSUNAMI: PORNOGRAPHY

Deep beneath the ocean, on December 26, 2004, the earth shook. Far off the coast of Sumatra, Indonesia, an earthquake that registered between 9.1 and 9.3 on the Richter scale—making it the second strongest ever measured—caused the ocean floor to move vertically.

That vertical movement started a barely perceptible wave in the deep ocean. In fact, open ocean ships moved right across the top of the wave and never noticed it.

As the wave got closer to shore, however, it hit shallower water and began to rise in height, ultimately to as much as one hundred feet. When the Indian Ocean tsunami hit shore, it destroyed everything in its path, buildings and people alike. That one event deep beneath the ocean set in motion a horrific process that eventually took the lives of more than 225,000 people in South and Southeast Asia.

There is another tsunami coming.

This one carries the same magnitude of potential destruction. It's a tsunami already positioned to wash over our culture. As ministry leaders we need to be aware, informed, and educated about the cause and be prepared to deal with the aftermath when it strikes. Hospital church ministries are—and will be—an integral tool in helping people deal with this massive wave of destruction.

## RIGHT AROUND THE CORNER

The tsunami I am referring to is the destruction to marriages and the family from pornography and the addiction that often results from it. It's rapidly moving beneath the surface, virtually undetected in many churches, but a huge wave is coming. A wave poised to destroy marriages and families.

One of the problems here is the secrecy that surrounds this addiction. It is almost a badge of honor in our culture to say that you are a recovering alcoholic. But there is no badge of honor that goes with saying you are a recovering sex addict. Many misconceptions cloud people's understanding of what being a sex addict means. They conjure up images of pedophiles snatching children off playgrounds, when the truth is, though all pedophiles are sex addicts, few sex addicts are pedophiles.

The vast majority of sex addicts are not criminals. They are men and women who use sex as a drug, the same way alcoholics or drug addicts use their drug. Make no mistake about it: sexual addicts are sitting in churches every Sunday morning. Week after week, they are teaching Sunday school, functioning as elders and deacons, and some are preaching in pulpits.

You would think that a hospital church ministry such as ours would have the greatest number of people in freedom groups for struggles related to drugs and alcohol, or perhaps for marriage and family issues—but our ministry to recovering sex addicts today is the largest and most consistently attended freedom group in our ministry. You heard that correctly: sexual addiction is number one. In these freedom groups, we minister to not only the addict but the spouse of the addict as well.

The issue of sexual addiction caught us unaware at first. All around us marriages began to fall apart, husbands started getting caught with pornography, in affairs, and visiting prostitutes, and we knew we had to do something. Although we were heavily involved in recovery ministry already, we knew very little about how to deal with the specific issue of sexual addiction. So we got informed, educated, and went to work.

After we had begun to have some success in ministering to families in this area, we decided it was time to bring the issue out into the full light of day. On September 21, 2003, we devoted a special Sunday to this issue entitled "The Day Celebration Told the Truth about Pornography." We had a panel discussion in the Sunday morning service where six couples and one single man told their stories. These were all people who were currently involved in recovery as sex addicts and who had received ministry and restoration in their marriages (if they were married). They told of the shame, frustration, despair, and destruction that goes along with this addiction, and how they had now found restoration within a transparent community dedicated to help, hope, and healing.

Interestingly, I didn't announce beforehand that this Sunday focus was going to happen. I knew if I did, there would be men and women who would find a convenient excuse to miss church that morning. So people showed up thinking it was going to be a normal Sunday worship experience. It was obvious to me that God was in this, because that morning we had the highest attendance we had ever experienced other than on an Easter Sunday. At the end of the service, I issued the challenge to get help. We were inundated by the response. From that day forward, we were off and running in ministering to men, women, and families caught in this area.

## STAGGERING NUMBERS

As bad as it is right now, this problem of sexual addiction is going to get much worse within the next decades. This tsunami is gathering strength.

The reason for this massive wave is the increased availability of and easy access to pornography because of the Internet. When I was growing up, a young man had to find a magazine that his father or a friend's father had hidden or somehow manage to steal a magazine from a store. He couldn't buy a magazine directly, and there was certainly no Internet then.

Today, pornography is as accessible as a computer screen or a cell phone and accessible to everyone—even kids and young people. Dr. Al Cooper, a pioneer in the study of cybersex, describes the Triple A Engine that drives Internet porn:

- Accessible (just a click of the mouse and you can see it)

- Affordable (much of it is free online)

- Anonymous (no one has to know you're watching it)[1]

These three factors have removed the traditional blocks between an individual and pornography. As these young men and women get married, have children, and the spiral of their addiction gets tighter and faster, the devastation on marriages, families, and the church is going to be massive. Bonnie Erbe, contributing editor at *U.S. News & World Report*, writes that as much as a third of the adult population regularly visits porn sites. "One of the Web's less admirable accomplishments is that it has allowed porn to propagate to a point once thought unimaginable. In the 1950s, could one in three Americans have visited a pornography shop? Of course not. But now it's accessible in your house, on your street, [and] at your local Internet café."[2]

Much research has been done in this area already, yet I feel the need to mention some of it for the convincing of those who might be skeptical about the depth of the problem. The Internet has opened the door to everything. That is both good and bad. We have instant access to information that just a few years ago only a handful at the top of the academic pyramid could gain access to. We have instant access to friends and family all around the globe. But along with the positive also comes instant access to everything destructive.

Consider these destructive effects of widespread instant access:

1. Al Cooper and Eric Griffin-Shelley, Introduction to *Sex and the Internet: A Guidebook for Clinicians*, ed. Al Cooper (New York: Brunner-Routlege, 2002), 5–6.
2. Bonnie Erbe, "Porn Is No Liberator," usnews.com opinion blog, June 6, 2007, http://www.usnews.com/blogs/erbe/2007/6/6/porn-is-no-liberator.html.

- The current average age of first exposure to pornography is 11 years of age. Some 80 percent of 15- to 17-year-olds report having had multiple hard-core exposures, and some 90 percent of 8- to 16-year-olds report having viewed pornography online. [3]

- Citing statistics from comScore, an internet traffic measuring service, Pamela Paul reports some 70 percent of 18- to 24-year-old men visit pornographic sites in a typical month; 66 percent of men in their twenties and thirties also report being regular users of pornography.[4]

- In 2002, Rick Warren, pastor of Saddleback Community Church, did a confidential survey of pastors visiting his Web site.[5] His survey revealed that a significant percentage, as many as 30 percent, of pastors struggled with Internet pornography. That's pastors! This isn't just a problem in the world. It is right here in our churches among pastors and believers.

- Annual porn revenue in the United States exceeds the combined annual revenues of ABC, CBS, and NBC. Porn revenue worldwide is larger than the revenues of the world's top technology companies combined. Just among the sixteen nations for which statistics were available, the pornography industry brought in 97.06 billion dollars in 2006. [6]

With billions of dollars in profit on the table, this thing isn't

3. Jerry Ropelato, "Internet Pornography Statistics," TopTenReviews.com, at http://internet-filter-review.toptenreviews.com/internet-pornography-statistics.html#anchor5.
4. Pamela Paul, *Pornified: How Pornography Is Transforming Our Lives, Our Relationships, and Our Families* (New York: Times Books, 2005) 15–16. This source was brought to my attention by a 2005 article in Baptist Press.
5. *Rick Warren's Ministry Toolbox* 49 (April 24, 2002).
6. "2006 and 2005 Pornography United States Industry Revenue Statistics" and "2006 Worldwide Pornography Revenues," www.familysafemedia.com/pornography_statistics.html.

going away. It is only going to get worse. Regardless of the social, personal, and cultural devastation that comes from it, as long as that much financial gain is at stake, there will be people who will continue to produce it and market it to anyone who will buy it.

Because of this, the tsunami is growing to huge proportions. When it hits the shore, the force of its destruction will take out individuals, marriages, and families. We in the body of Christ need to be better informed about its enormity, and better prepared to begin dealing with it now and when the full force of it hits in a few years.

## A DIFFICULT SUBJECT

I have found that ministering in this area of addiction is the most difficult of all addictions. As difficult as alcohol and drug addiction are, in my experience they are not nearly as difficult to address as sexual addiction. There are reasons why this is true. Sexual addiction is difficult to address because of: its secret nature, its shameful nature, its sexual nature, and its widespread prevalence. Let's look at each of these more closely. These reasons are the same reasons why we must put sexual addiction at the top of our list of things to address in the church.

### *Its secret nature*

An alcoholic will show signs of drunkenness, such as slurred speech or staggering walk. A drug addict will show signs of being high, such as dilated pupils or dulled mood, or paraphernalia or drugs will be found, track marks (if used intravenously) can be seen, blood can be tested, breath can be smelled, and the like.

Yet, this is not true for the sex addict. There are most often no physical signs of sex addiction and the use of pornography. With the advent of the Internet there isn't even a paper trail anymore. The addict doesn't need to buy magazines or videos that might be found by a spouse, family member, or friend. Everything can be accessed electronically, and then the history of the computer wiped away, leaving no evidence at all. No doubt, sex addicts do sometimes get caught using their computer at work or at home, but for every one that is caught there are thousands who are never detected.

This very truth contributes to the epidemic nature of sex addiction already in our culture, and to its increasingly epidemic nature in the coming generations. When a teenager begins to experiment with drugs or alcohol, the opportunity for perceptive parents to discover it and intervene is almost always there. Physical signs and other indicators such as a drop in grades, a lack of interest in normal activities, a change in friends can be detected. But with pornography, those outward indications are not necessarily there. Pornography is viewed in secret, no peer group is necessary, grades need not be affected, and normal activities continue. A teen can be moving down the path to sexual addiction and still be a straight A student, homecoming king, captain of the football team, the most popular kid in school, and leader of his church youth group. So the opportunity to discover it and intervene before the addictive cycle has tightened is much less than with any other addiction. Add to this a basic ignorance and skepticism about the prevalence of pornography use, and you have a formula for disaster.

Recently, a friend I grew up with who is now a pastor did something in a Sunday morning worship service that blew the lid off the secret in his church. I don't know if I would recommend it or not, but it was a gutsy move, and it illustrated what's really going on in the lives of many teens.

In the morning service, my friend asked all the kids in the service to go sit beside their parents. They were reluctant but with some strong encouragement eventually all of them did what he asked. Then he told the kids whose parents weren't there to go sit beside an adult. When everyone was in place, he told all the kids to get out their cell phones. Again there was reluctance, but he said they would be there all day until every cell phone was out. Then he told them to turn the phones off. When all phones were off, he told them to give them to their parents or to the adult with whom they were sitting. Reluctantly the kids relinquished their phones. Once the adults had the phones, he told them to turn the phones back on. Kids' eyes got wide as they began to suspect a problem. Then he told the parents to go to the text messages on their kids' phones and read the messages they had been sending and receiving from their friends. When he said that, kids began to scramble to get their phones back as parents held them away. There was bedlam in the church as parents began to read the sexually explicit messages that some of their kids had on their phones. There were gasps of shock from some and outbursts of tears and wailing from others. Naive parents couldn't believe the things their kids were saying back and forth, and the pictures they were sending, not only with their school friends but church friends as well.

The sad thing is that these were Christian kids, in a small, tight-knit community. Many were active in their church youth group, in church two or three times per week, and going on weekend spiritual retreats and summer camp. The whole deal. The church was located in the kind of community where people go to get away from the evils of the urban environment. They want to raise their family in a safe, clean, and wholesome place.

I bet that if that same experiment was done in virtually any church in America today, the results would be about the same. Parents would be shocked. Kids would be embarrassed. The dirty secrets would be revealed. (Remember: secrets are bullets in the Enemy's gun.)

### Its shameful nature

There is much more shame attached to sexual addiction than any other addiction. This shame not only contributes to the addiction's continued secrecy but also contributes to its continued practice. Shame will prevent an addict from seeking help because he is ashamed to speak about the problem. Sadly, the very shame attached to it will keep driving the addict back to it. That sounds insane, but all addiction at its root is insane.

Here's how the cycle works: The use of pornography creates shame in a person. Then, that shame makes a person feel bad, and that "down" feeling drives a person back to the "high" feeling that comes with their drug. The cycle becomes self-perpetuating. This is why the addictive cycle gets tighter over time and usually escalates in more overt behavior the longer it continues. The proverbial dog chases his tail until he drops from exhaustion.

Sex is still the subject that parents have the most reluctance to speak about with their children, and it is still the subject that the church is least likely to speak about openly. Even with all of the sexual openness in our secular culture, there is still an unwillingness to speak about sex openly and honestly in families and in the church. We all know sex happens, because none of us would be here without it, but it isn't a subject that most parents, pastors, and churches feel free to speak about and educate about openly. Therefore, the ignorance about the problem of sex addiction continues, and the church continues to do nothing about ministering in this area because of embarrassment and shame. Even in the Hospital Church, when I speak about this issue openly, some parents are uncomfortable about their kids hearing it. Yet kids are already hearing about it on the playground, in the locker room, and on the Internet. The information they are getting in those places is often twisted, secular, and destructive. If we don't tell them the truth in the church, where are they going to hear it?

Several years ago, Shannon Ethridge spoke at a weekend youth retreat at the Hospital Church on the subject of sexual purity. Shannon is the author of *Every Woman's Battle*, which is the woman's side of the issue that Stephen Arterburn and Fred Stoeker wrote about in *Every Man's Battle*. Shannon is a champion for sexual purity and integrity. She speaks frankly and openly about issues of sex and the church's need to address this issue.

After she finished speaking with our teens, she remarked to me about how mature they seemed to be about the subject. There wasn't any of the usual snickering, looking down, and nervous laughter that she normally encounters with teenage groups. I told her it was because in the Hospital Church we talk about the subject openly and hopefully without shame and embarrassment. I was glad that she noticed a difference in our group. It indicates that we are at least making an attempt to deal with the issue. Shannon has become a great friend and supporter of the Hospital Church and the ministry we do.

### Its sexual nature

One thing that makes sex addiction so difficult to deal with, and overcome, is that it has to do with a normal bodily function—sex. God has created us as sexual creatures. The sexual expression is part of how He made us and intends for us to live. But alcohol is not a part of our nature, nor are drugs. An alcoholic can quit drinking and never drink alcohol again. A drug addict can quit cocaine and never do cocaine again. This is because God didn't create us with a desire, or need for, alcohol or cocaine. But sex is different.

When a sex addict enters into recovery for his or her sexual addiction, he or she is still a sexual creature with a natural sexual need and desire. If the person is married, then God's intention is that he or she experience sex in the way God intended with his or her spouse. If the person is single, God's standard is abstinence until marriage. The struggle for the addict is to recover from the addiction and separate the addiction from the normal, natural, God-honoring expression of sex between a husband and a wife. This can be difficult and confusing for the recovering person.

It is a similar problem faced by a person with a food addiction. You still have to eat in a way that is healthy for the body as God created us. Food is a basic need that God created within us. Abstinence from food isn't an option. But once a person's use of sex or food has gotten warped and twisted into an unhealthy and destructive obsession, all the wires get crossed, definitions are twisted, reality is warped, and the recovery process requires a great deal of diligence, help, and accountability.

### Its widespread prevalence

In our culture, we are surrounded by sex everywhere we go. Sex is used to sell everything from toothpaste to automobiles. A widespread number of highway billboards, magazine advertisements, and television commercials contain sexual images or ideas. The *Dick Van Dyke* show of decades past wouldn't even show Dick Van Dyke and his wife in the show, Mary Tyler Moore, sleeping in the same bed. Yet, now we have commercials for Victoria's Secret shown on network television at 8:00 in the evening. The stuff shown in the Victoria's Secret commercials would have been considered soft porn not too many years ago. These images are difficult enough for *any* person to deal with, without them leading to obsessive thoughts about sex. How much more for the person who is trying to unravel years of sexual addiction, or for teenagers who are dealing with raging adolescent hormones?

## A CHEMICAL PROBLEM ALSO

Dr. Dean Belnap, a board certified psychiatrist with thirty years of practice in the field of child neuropsychiatry, is currently a member of the clinical faculty at the University of Utah medical school and has done extensive research in sex addiction. He writes about how it's the euphoric effect of drugs upon the pleasure center of the brain (the limbic system) that creates an addictive need that has essentially the same effect upon the brain that is experienced in sexual addiction. When any brain, but particularly the developing adolescent brain, is bombarded with sexual images it can quickly become addicted within the limbic system. In effect, he says, people lose the prefrontal cortex control in their brains. "The change is manifest in every aspect of their lives: relationships, values, and purpose are up for grabs as the brain downshifts to dependency and need."[7]

A few years ago, another clinical psychologist, Dr. Jeffrey Satinover, was one of several authorities that spoke before a Senate subcommittee on the effects of pornography on the brain, families, and communities. Dr. Satinover spoke at length about the chemical and addictive nature of pornography:

> It may seem surprising that, at this juncture, I should speak of chemicals, when one might be thinking instead of sex.

---

7. W. Dean Belnap, "Can Negative Imprinting Be Reversed?" March 2, 2005, part 2 of 10 in A Brain Gone Wrong series, *Meridian Magazine*, http://www.meridianmagazine.com/ideas/050111brain2.html issue 109.

But, in fact, modern science allows us to understand that the underlying nature of an addiction to pornography is chemically nearly identical to a heroin addiction: Only the delivery system is different, and the sequence of steps. That is why heroin addicts in particular give up sex and routinely compare their "rushes" to "orgasms."

The chemistry involved is as follows: Upon viewing or reading the "expression," the pornography addict experiences an irresistible impulse to self-stimulation. Not so upon reading Melville, or Batman, or *The Washington Post*. For the addict, this impulse has become more intense from pornography than from people he loves or who love him and requires ever more extreme forms of pornographic expression to achieve the same level of pleasure.

Upon achieving climax, the brain releases opioids— chemicals that are the naturally occurring analogs to synthetic opiates such as morphine or heroin. It is to ever higher levels of these opioids that the pornography addict has become addicted in tandem with the delivery system that ensures their release. Indeed, he—and today, with the Internet, in ever increasing numbers, she—has become part of that delivery system—along with the pornographic "expression" itself. The pornography addict soon forgets about everything and everyone else in favor of an ever more elusive sexual jolt. He will eventually be able to find it only among other junkies like himself, and he will place at risk his career, his friends, his family. He will indulge his habit anywhere and everywhere, at any time. No one, no matter how highly placed, is immune. And like all other addicts, the pornography addict will lie to cover it up, heedless of risk or cost to himself or to others."[8]

Viewing sexual addiction in light of its chemical nature may

---

8. Jeffrey Satinover, Hearing on the Brain Science Behind Pornography Addiction and the Effects of Addiction on Families and Communities, Senate Committee on Commerce, Science and Transportation, Subcommittee on Science, Technology and Space, November 18, 2004, http://obscenitycrimes.org/Senate-Reisman-Layden-Etc.pdf.

be a new concept for many. So I want to show several other studies that back up these findings. As ministers, it's not that we need to shift the responsibility of overcoming a sexual addiction away from the individual. Simply, we need to know that when a person views porn, his brain gets messed up chemically. So we're not dealing with a bad habit that needs to be overcome but a chemical craving as well.

This chemical component to sexual addiction wreaks havoc on a marriage. One of the most problematic effects of pornography addiction is the devastating effect it has upon an individual's ability to experience true intimacy with one's spouse. This is one of the major contributing factors to marriage separation when pornography becomes involved. An explanation of this effect can be found in the following statement:

> When someone views pornography, neuroscientists can observe how the brain releases dopamine. This is the primary hormone released during cocaine use. This is also the hormone that is naturally released in otherwise normal sexual or romantic encounters. When viewing porn, the brain also releases oxytocin. This is a strong hormone that is also released the first time mothers and fathers hold their newborn baby or when lovers hold hands. Oxytocin creates a bonding effect. The brain simply can't distinguish between viewing pornography and a sexual encounter, so these hormones are released. But instead of bonding to another person, the brain is bonding to pornographic images and opening the viewer up to a dopamine addiction. Pornography is essentially overexposure to erotic stimuli that exhausts our normal sexual responses.[9]

Recently Jill Manning, a university sociologist, testified before a United States Senate Committee on the topic of "Why the

---

9. Luke Gilkerson, "Teens and Internet Pornography (Part 1)." Originally found at www.covenanteyes.com; accessed at http://www.creatinggreathomes.com/public/235.cfm?sd=21 in April 2009.

Government Should Care about Pornography." She assured the committee that her talk was not based upon anecdotal evidence or personal views but upon the findings of established studies that had been published in peer-reviewed journals. She revealed the established negative impacts of pornography on intimacy in marriage, marital distress, and divorce, and a list of other devastating results upon marriages and children who are raised in a home where pornography is used.

Manning told the committee:

> Research reveals many systemic effects of Internet pornography that are undermining an already vulnerable culture of marriage and family. Even more disturbing is the fact that the first Internet generations have not reached full maturity, so the upper limits of this impact have yet to be realized.
>
> I am convinced that Internet pornography is grooming young generations of Americans in such a way that their chances of enjoying healthy and enduring relationships are handicapped.[10]

Manning's line is very sobering: "the upper limits of this impact have yet to be realized." This is the tsunami I'm talking about. The Internet—and the unprecedented access to porn it brings—is too new for anyone to know the exact effect so much porn will have upon society in the coming years.

### WHAT CAN BE DONE?

We must begin preparations now in two key areas: prevention and treatment.[11] We must teach, educate, and inform. We

---

10. Jill Manning, "Why the Government Should Care about Pornography," Hearing on Pornography's Impact on Marriage and the Family, Testimony before the United States Senate Committee on the Judiciary, Subcommittee on the Constitution, Civil Rights and Property Rights, November 9, 2005, http://judiciary.senate.gov/hearings/testimony.cfm?id=1674&wit_id=4826.

11. Three solid ministries that provide specific help and materials are www.purityproject.org; www.operationintegrity.com; and www.prodigalsonline.org

need to blow away the secrecy of this addiction once and for all. We need to spread the word that porn destroys. It is not a harmless behavioral pattern undertaken by normal, responsible adults in the privacy of their own houses—that idea is a complete fallacy.

Pornography, and its chemically addictive component, begins by offering a false solution to life's problems. As people increasingly turn to porn to get a rush that falsely tells them that life is better, the need for more and more pornography (and harder types of it) increasingly escalates. The chemically addictive component of pornography alters the brain's chemistry and creates illogical cravings inside people's brains. Porn hampers normal sexual development of young people, as well as normal sexual activity between husbands and wives. Plain and simple, pornography hurts people and destroys families.

For those who are already caught in this addiction, we must give opportunity for confession, treatment, accountability, and hope. Again, like any other addiction, the path to wholeness is found in community, transparency, and forgiveness of root issues—all subjects we have already looked at in this book.

Ultimate recovery seldom happens overnight. As people are in the freedom group process, we can help them in this area by providing systems of community that provide daily accountability and boundary setting.

This is a war we can win. The battle is not against people. Never. It is a battle for people's lives and souls.

The wave has gathered force and is ready to hit shore soon. Are we ready?

# PART SIX

# The Beginning

CHAPTER 11

# WIIERE TO GO FROM HERE

As I am writing this chapter I'm imagining a pastor or church leader who has read all that's been written to this point and says to himself, "I'm sold! I'm ready to get started. Where do I start? How do I begin? What do I do first, and second, and third . . . Give me a plan!"

I certainly understand that enthusiasm and am thankful for it. However, as I've said several places in this book, I am hesitant to give a specific plan. There isn't a one-size-fits-all plan for how to do this, and my reason for writing this book is not so you can make another Celebration Fellowship. Situations, communities, leaders, and congregations are different. Work to apply the principles presented in this book to the specific needs and dynamics of your own congregation. Your church will—and should—look different from mine.

That being said, there are, however, some basic principles that I am convinced have application in all settings. They are broad principles that have for the most part been learned from my own failures and sometimes, by the grace of God, the failures of others. I hope to give you the benefit of the lessons that I and others have learned so you won't have to repeat all the same mistakes.

I'll make this last section as practical as I can.

## START SLOW AND SMALL

I know this can be hard to hear for hard-driving, kingdom-oriented pastors (particularly entrepreneurial-minded church planters who need to push hard to survive)—Rome wasn't built in a day. Rome began small, with a dream and a vision, and over the course of centuries grew to the height of its prominence. Even the vision of what Rome was grew as the city grew into an empire. Relax. Start small, and allow the Lord to lead you into this new phase of ministry.

What happens when you run ahead of God's plans? Remember the dot-com surge and fall of 1995–2001? Rome might not have been built in a day, but this thing was. The "dot-com bubble" refers to a wildly speculative few years when stock markets in Western nations saw their value increase rapidly from growth in the new Internet sector and related fields. The period was marked by the founding (and, in many cases, spectacular failure) of a group of new Internet-based companies referred to as dot-coms.

Almost overnight the entire industry cropped up and seemed to dominate the investment landscape. Stock values went from pennies to hundreds of dollars, in some cases, in a matter of weeks. The problem is that most of it was built upon hype, excitement, and mass hysteria. Beneath the surface there was little real value undergirding the stock prices. Some of these dot-coms didn't even produce anything tangible—they weren't much more than a Web site and a name that had been incorporated and offered in a public stock option. When the crash came, the bubble burst hard and fast.

Most things in history that have made a lasting impact took time to create. Some of them faced opposition at first because they challenged the paradigms through which people viewed the world. That was true with the advent of the automobile. It took people time to adjust to this new idea of travel. Travel used to be by horse, or buggy, or train, or foot. Now we can't imagine life without our wheels. The same was true when Alexander Graham Bell introduced the telephone. People couldn't see how it would ever have practical widespread use. Today we carry one with us everywhere we go and can't imagine life without it.

Any new program in a church can be implemented in an instant. Just announce the program, buy the materials, sign people up, and you're on your way. But hospital church ministry isn't a program, it's a paradigm shift. People have to begin to see the church, ministry, spiritual maturity, and themselves through a new paradigm (actually through God's original one), all of which takes time. My experience is that the quickest way to destroy a church, divide a fellowship, and defeat a vision is to impose anything that sounds like a big new scary program on people. They will invariably be overwhelmed with it, resist the change, then often turn and actively fight against it, even when it is the right thing to do and you can show them chapter and verse to make your case. People behave this way whenever their paradigms are challenged quickly, rather than given space to change over the course of time.

More great ideas have died an agonizing death in the boiling pot of impatience than anything else. A leader goes to a conference and gets all pumped up, or reads a book and has an aha moment and races back to his church expecting everyone to be as fired up about it as he is. When they aren't immediately willing to embrace his enthusiasm, the leader labels them as hard-hearted, unspiritual, and traditionalists. Some of those descriptions might be true of some congregations, but more often than not the problem is an impatient and unwise leader who is unwilling to bring people lovingly and patiently through a paradigm shift.

Recently I was driving down a street that's without a doubt the most frustrating street to drive in my city. It's packed with traffic and has a traffic light every block or so. I spotted a guy who was obviously in a rush. He zipped by me and wove in and out of traffic only to get stopped at the next light. I soon pulled up next to him at the same light. When the light turned green, he zoomed out of the starting gate like Mario Andretti, weaving in and out of lanes again, burning rubber, not signaling, racing as fast as he could on the busy street.

Then, when I got to the next red light, there he sat again. Again, the light turned green. Again he zoomed off. Again, I met up with him at the next light.

This happened for four lights!

Then, before we got to the fifth light, he whipped out of his lane one time too many. Another car was making a lane shift from the other side, and they crashed.

I came puttering by, saw that no one was injured, and since there was nothing I could do, I went on my merry way. When I pulled into my driveway some time later I thought to myself of all the wasted effort of the man who had crashed. All his hurrying hadn't gotten him anywhere except in a mess. Yet I had made it safe and sound to my destination, which was the goal all along.

You have to decide which kind of leader you want to be—the steady and mature driver who gets where he wants to go, or the impatient young hotdog who crashes and burns.

Over the years that we have been doing this kind of ministry, we have expanded into having freedom groups that meet at a minimum of four different times per week. We have Wednesday and Thursday night groups. We have Saturday morning groups and Sunday morning groups. We offer somewhere in the neighborhood of fifteen different types of freedom groups ranging from men who are addicted to pornography to women who are survivors of sexual abuse and everything in between.

But in the beginning we only had one group. Just one. From that one group we have expanded as leadership, opportunity, and our awareness of need has expanded. It has been natural growth not artificial or program growth.

## COME ON IN AND STAY A WHILE

I grew up in West Texas, and "come on in and stay a while" was a very common greeting when folks showed up at your door for an unannounced visit. You invited them in, and they stayed a while. Sometimes they sat a long while. But it was usually a good time.

As I said earlier, when it comes to ministry, paradigm shifts often need to take place, and that takes time. If any leader intends to implement a shift, he or she should have the courage, patience, and integrity to make a commitment to stay a while.

It has always been intriguing and saddening to me that the average length of stay for a senior pastor in a church is only about two years.[1] That means that every few years a new leader comes in with new ideas, new strategies, new vision and direction. This is part of the reason why change is so difficult to implement in churches. They don't expect a leader to hang around for very long, so why should they let him come in and shake up their world?

I'm reminded of the story of the new pastor who came in all excited about things he wanted to do until the chairman of the deacons pulled him aside one day and explained the program to him. He said, "Pastor, we were here when you got here, and we'll still be here when you are gone. So you just do the preachin', and you leave runnin' the church to us, okay?" Now even if that isn't ever said out loud, there is no doubt that in churches where there is a revolving door of pastoral leadership, it is the understood rule.

I say this not to brag but as fact: I have been in pastoral ministry now for more than thirty-five years, twenty-eight of which have been as a senior pastor. In those twenty eight years I have served only two churches. My first one for three years out of seminary and at this writing twenty-five years at Celebration Fellowship. When I left my first church out of seminary to come here it was a move of starting over. It wasn't a step up the ministry ladder but a step down. When I made the move I committed myself to spend the rest of my ministry life there if the Lord would allow me to. (Isn't it interesting how God never seems to call a pastor to a smaller church? It always seems to be the next step up the ministry ladder.)

I would challenge any leader who is hard-charging up the ministry ladder not to consider beginning a hospital church ministry. Just "do the preachin', and leave the leadin' of the church to the people." You won't be in your current church long enough to earn the people's respect in any substantive way anyway. If

---

1. Michael J. Anthony and Mick Boersma, *Moving On, Moving Forward* (Grand Rapids: Zondervan, 2007), 14.

you try to implement widespread paradigm shifts, all you'll do is cause chaos and pain that the people will have to pay the price for long after you have moved on to greener pastures.

Stay a while.

That's my true encouragement. I don't know about you, but I would rather live in a house that I built rather than one someone else built and lived in first. Certainly I would rather live in a house that I built than a house that twenty others before me had lived in and each one added on his little section to the house according to his own taste. Isn't that what many churches look like today—a hodgepodge of additions have been tacked on over the course of the past forty years by fifteen different pastoral leaders? Some churches today are no more than a bunch of small additions connected one to another that in the end have created a monstrosity that no one can understand or explain.

## PRACTICE SAFE CHURCH

I heard once about the little boy who had been hearing about "safe sex" in school. He asked his granddaddy, "Papa, in your day what did you wear to practice safe sex?" His granddaddy held up his hand and said, "A wedding ring." Sound wisdom for every generation.

A wedding ring is for two people when they are both convinced of the sincerity of each other's commitment. They are set free to be themselves without fear. I have been wearing a wedding ring now for thirty years. I meant my vows when I said them, and so did my wife. We have proven that to each other repeatedly over these thirty years together. That sense of security in each other has created a safe place to be honest and real with each other.

The same is true with church. You've already read about how churches can become safe places. Practice those principles with the goal of your church becoming as transparent as a patient wearing a hospital gown, a place where people aren't all that concerned with the back being carefully closed and tied.

In review, the main points to creating a safe church are:

- Find a balance between law and license.

- Model transparency from the top down.

- Let people live their stories and then tell their stories.

- Give priority in programming to hospital ministry.

We've been asked before if we allow people with addictive backgrounds to serve in positions of leadership. The answer is yes. We have leaders who were former addicts to chemicals, sex, food—you name it. They come from all walks of life—professionals such as doctors and lawyers, business people, corporate executives, and minimum wage laborers.

When they come into church leadership, they understand that they must continue to do the things that gave them victory in the first place. If they stumble and act out in their addiction, then how do we act toward them in grace? I know what law and license do. Law condemns and judges and drives a person out in shame. License does nothing. It just ignores it because it isn't really a problem because there aren't any real boundaries established.

Grace does something! We have created an environment where a person in leadership who stumbles in sobriety can come clean about that stumble, admit it, and if the situation warrants, accept the need to step back from their position of leadership for a period of time to get reestablished in integrity. This applies to anyone in leadership: elders, teachers, praise team, drama team, and even the technical team that runs the lighting and computers for the Sunday worship service. This isn't about punishment. It's about loving discipline and integrity.

Do we ever have situations where someone is unwilling to accept loving discipline? Yes, sadly, we do. Several times the elders needed to take formal action to remove someone from the church who was unwilling to accept loving discipline. He or she wanted to continue behavior that dishonored God, self, and the body of Christ. To protect the reputation of the ministry, formal action had to be taken to remove them from the church, but only after every possible attempt had been made to bring the person to his or her senses. The door is always open for the person to come in humble repentance and find restoration. We have had that happen, and it is always a cause for joyful celebration when real grace wins out over law or license.

Each body of believers needs to develop principles for how these situations will be handled. I emphasize principles, not policies. Policies are more rigid. My experience is that as soon as I make a policy, something is going to happen that the policy doesn't fit without violating a person. Principles are established from Scripture and allow the leadership of the Holy Spirit in how they are applied in each unique situation. Principles keep us from violating God's Word and from violating people. Principles guide us to act how Jesus acted in John 8 with the woman caught in adultery. He didn't condemn her, but neither did He ignore her sin. God's Word was honored and so was the person.

## CHOOSE A FACILITATOR

If you begin with one freedom group, then you have to begin with one facilitator. After years of freedom group work, we now have the benefit of being able to set rigorous standards people must meet before they facilitate a group. In the beginning, we didn't have that luxury. When you start from scratch, you do the best you can with the resources you have, and God honors that.

When we decided to move in this direction, I had one man in my church who I knew had some freedom group experience. He was my friend Chuck, about whom I have spoken previously. Chuck had been an executive with a major U.S. automobile manufacturer and had taken early retirement at the age of fifty-eight. Within weeks of retirement, he entered a treatment center for his alcoholism. Soon after he got out of treatment, he came to know Christ as Savior. One Sunday morning, he and his wife showed up at the school where our church was meeting at the time. Chuck continued his recovery in his AA group outside the church, and he began to grow in Christ through the ministry inside the church.

One day I tapped Chuck on the shoulder and asked him if he would be willing to take his knowledge of the freedom group process and apply it to begin a group within the church. He agreed. We found a biblically based twelve-step workbook, put out the word, and started a group. Chuck did an excellent job. From that first group we have grown and expanded to other groups and facilitators. Chuck eventually came on my staff in a volunteer capacity to coordinate our entire freedom group ministry.

We now have the luxury of requiring that someone complete at least one freedom groups personally and then co-facilitate at least two groups before being put into the position of lead facilitator. That is an excellent plan and process, but that isn't where we started. We worked with what we had and moved forward.

Just about every church in America has someone who is in recovery through Alcoholics Anonymous, Narcotics Anonymous, Sex and Love Addicts Anonymous, or any number of other types of recovery/support groups. These people can be a resource for beginning a freedom group ministry, because they have already been exposed to the concepts of what freedom groups are and what they are not. They understand how freedom groups function and the basic guidelines that apply to a freedom group. Those are different from community home groups or Bible study groups. The rules are different, the guidelines are different, and the purposes are different. In order to have success, those things need to be understood and respected.

Without going through an extensive facilitator training manual here (which we now have at Celebration), let me mention a few things that are important to know about the groups and about facilitators.

- Freedom groups are not counseling groups. A freedom group is where people walk through a process individually and together and support one another as the Holy Spirit guides each person's own pilgrimage of growth and healing.

- Freedom groups are not advice groups. In fact, giving advice is not allowed in the freedom group process. What individuals do is share their own "experience, strength, and hope" with one another. When someone asks a question in a group, that is not an invitation for the group to begin giving advice. It is an invitation for others in the group to share their experience. To share about how they have found strength or hope in a similar situation. If a person does not have "experience, strength, or hope" to share that is appropriate to the question or situation, then they should be silent. Advice giving is behavior that will destroy a group quickly. This guideline is important because people in a freedom group process are not counselors, teachers, or advisors. They are fellow members who are there to grow, discover, support, and be supported.

- Facilitators are not counselors, teachers, or advisors. They are facilitators, or guides for the process. The facilitators share their "experience, strength, and hope" just like any other member when it is appropriate. The facilitator is there to keep the group moving in the direction of the material the group is using and to monitor the group so that the group guidelines are adhered to and respected. There are times when the facilitator has to manage conflict in the group, encourage members to share honestly, or even confront lovingly when someone is acting in an inappropriate way that is not conducive to the health and purpose of the group.

In general, the facilitator does all of these things and more in order to promote a loving, caring, trusting environment where people will feel safe to share their secrets, struggles, and successes.

It has been our experience that the success or failure of a group (and that is measured by the growth and healing of persons in the group) is most often tied to the quality of the facilitator and how well he or she does the job of facilitating. There are people who are gifted at facilitating a freedom group, and there are people who are gifted at teaching or preaching. The two are not often found in the same person. I am the first to admit that my strength is not as a facilitator. I am a teacher, and it is difficult for me when I am facilitating a group to keep from taking on the teacher role. I talk too much. For that reason, I typically don't facilitate groups anymore. It frustrates me, and I have to constantly keep a hold on myself. I'm just not very good at it. My contribution to the process now is to train and equip facilitators, and in recent years to write and develop biblically based, Christ-honoring material for the groups. There are plenty of others in the body who are very good at facilitating. Once you begin the ministry, you will find them. They will become evident.

## ASK FOR HELP WHERE YOU NEED IT

When we began this work some twenty years ago, we didn't have, or at least we didn't know of, any resources to help us. We stumbled along, and by the grace of God we learned. Along the way we made many mistakes that could have been avoided if we had known someone who could mentor us in the beginning. This solitude in ministry is no longer a necessity. There are many in the body of Christ who are doing wonderful ministry in this area and are willing to help, train, and encourage churches in the process. One of the greatest blessings for me in recent years has been to have the privilege of guiding other churches who understood the need and wanted to enter in.

We are so committed to this type of ministry now that our church has made a commitment that in church planting, we will only plant a church that is willing to be a hospital church ministry. Any church that is willing to become a refuge will find us and others like us ready and willing to come alongside and give everything we can to smooth the way.

I have made a commitment to spend the next season of my ministry writing, teaching, mentoring, and training others about this kind of ministry, as I continue to lead Celebration Fellowship. To that end, if I can be of any help either long distance or on-site in your place of ministry, feel free to contact me at James@Jamesmreeves.com. I would be honored and blessed to be an encouragement and resource for you wherever you are.

## WELCOME TO THE BEGINNING

As I write these final pages, I am reminded once again of the importance and blessing of this ministry. Just this week a woman in my congregation died in childbirth. This was her third child. Doctors aren't quite sure yet what happened, but the woman either had a brain aneurism or developed a blood clot during labor. Her death was instant, and efforts to revive her proved fruitless. When medical personnel were convinced their efforts were in vain, they saved the baby by emergency C-section.

Interestingly, this woman came to us several years ago specifically because she was hurting and needed help. She wasn't a down-and-out person. She was an intelligent, bright, and witty personality. But she was wounded and had recognized that she needed healing. She came to us specifically because she had been told that we were that kind of place. Then she came to Christ. She got involved in the healing process and began to grow in true emotional and spiritual maturity and became involved in the ministry.

In the room with her the moment she died were two women of the church who had walked through that process with her. One of them called me the moment it happened, from the hospital room, even while the medical team was still attempting to revive her.

By the time I arrived, there were already ten to twelve others there before me. More people in the process. More people who had deep and lasting connections with her because of the things they had shared and experienced together. This was not just church. This was community. Real community.

This Saturday we will gather for her memorial service. There will be sadness, without a doubt. She was a bright light in our midst, and her death came so suddenly and so tragically during the giving of a new life. But there will also be so much genuine rejoicing. She had lived out her last few years in such wholeness. Where would she be if she had not found help?

Where will so many others be if they do not find a refuge in the body of Christ? Thank you, Stacy, for letting us be a part of your life. Thank you for being a part of ours. We will be here for your family just as we were here for you and you were here for others. And we look forward to that day when there will be no more tears or sadness. No more death or dying. When we will be like Him for we shall see Him as He is.

Pastoral work is seldom easy.

But it can be wonderful.

That's what developing a hospital church ministry can do.

I pray that this book has been an encouragement, a challenge, and even a revelation to you. May God bless you, guide you, and empower you as you seek to transform your body of believers into a refuge, a place of help, hope, and healing.

# Suggested Curriculum for Freedom Groups

This is by no means a comprehensive list of the excellent biblically based materials that are available, nor is it an exhaustive list of the materials utilized at Celebration Fellowship. However, it is a list of some of the key materials that any church can immediately have access to and begin to utilize.

Littlefield, Cynthia Kubetin, and James Mallory. *Shelter from the Storm.* Nashville: LifeWay, 1995.

This is a workbook designed for survivors of sexual abuse. The trauma that sexual abuse perpetrates upon an individual cannot be overstated. This workbook is designed to help survivors learn to be free from the haunting memories of their abuse and feel physically, spiritually, and emotionally whole again.

McGee, Robert S. *The Search for Significance: Build Your Self-Worth on God's Truth.* Nashville: LifeWay, 2004.

This workbook is designed to help the participant begin to define self-worth and value in Christ. We all seek for significance, but often we look for it in all the wrong places. This is a solidly biblical process for discovering our worth and value in Christ.

Prodigals International. www.iprodigals.com.

Prodigals international provides training and materials for freedom groups focused on sexual addiction recovery. Before people can use the Prodigals material they must have gone through the Prodigals training. This is the process that is used at Celebration Fellowship and has been extremely helpful in our ministry. Information for training and materials can be found at their Web site. Other well-respected ministries in the area of sexual addiction recovery can be reached at www.thepurityproject.org and www.operationintegrity.com.

Reeves, James M. *The ABCs of Life Change*, and *The ABCs of Life Change for Couples*, Self-published. (Available at www.jamesmreeves.com.)

This is an intensely practical, biblically based twelve-step workbook that is designed for any Christian who desires life change in any area. This workbook was developed and implemented at Celebration Fellowship, the Hospital Church. At its core is the truth of the emotional-spiritual principle. (Please note: The outline for this workbook is available on my Web site for free. To order the complete workbook, please contact me through the Web site.)

Sledge, Tim. *Making Peace with Your Past*. Nashville: LifeWay, 1992.

This is a general workbook to help the person who grew up in a dysfunctional family identify the effects that environment has had on his or her life. When these issues are identified, then the participant can move into other groups that deal specifically with the struggles he or she has identified.

Springle, Pat. *Conquering Codependency*. Nashville: LifeWay, 1993.

This workbook is a biblically based twelve-step process specifically designed for persons who are obsessive people-pleasers and have difficulty seeing themselves as a person of worth and value apart from the approval of others. Issues such as perfectionism and a tendency to withdraw from others are also addressed.

# About the Hospital Church

The Hospital Church is the nickname given to Celebration Fellowship, an innovative Christ-following church in Fort Worth, Texas, led by Dr. James M. Reeves.

Founded in 1984, the church transitioned to a freedom group model in 1992 to help facilitate wholeness in all people. The church has since grown to a membership of 1,600 with two worship services and two Bible study hours on Sunday morning.

Celebration is actively involved in helping other churches implement hospital church ministry wherever they can. Our vision is that churches should become places of refuge to deal with the hurts of life. Too often churches have turned their backs on people looking to struggle through and recover from the problems brought on by childhood pain or bad choices. Celebration's vision is to help develop churches into the very places that people should be able to turn to for help, hope, and healing.

For more information, see the following Web sites:

www.thehospitalchurch.com
www.jamesmreeves.com

# ABOUT THE AUTHOR

As senior pastor of Fort Worth's 1,600-member Celebration Fellowship, Dr. James M. Reeves regularly sees wounded people find hope and restoration through Jesus Christ.

After receiving his B.A. in Greek from Baylor University in 1976, James received his M.Div. and D.Min. degrees from Southwestern Baptist Theological Seminary in 1981 and 1988.

He has been a pastor for more than thirty years with the past twenty-eight years in senior pastor positions. Twenty-five years have been in the same church, Celebration Fellowship, which James came to soon after it was planted. For the past eighteen years, that church has practiced hospital church ministry.

James is no stranger to recovery circles. He was born into an alcoholic home and suffered the emotional wounds of a rough childhood. Years later, the bills began to come due in his life as the emotional wounds that he had glossed over and ignored for years began to surface. James nearly resigned from pastoral ministry but chose to confront his past, then used his new-found freedom in Christ to build a church based on resolving emotional woundedness issues for greater intimacy with God.

Today, in addition to his responsibilities at Celebration Fellowship, James speaks at seminars and mentors other churches seeking to make similar transitions to the hospital church model.

James and his wife, Laura, live near Fort Worth and have two grown children: Tiffany, a pediatric trauma intensive care nurse at Children's Medical Center in Dallas, and Zack, a professional golfer.

If you would like to have James come speak for your conference or do on site training at your church, or if you would like more info on how you can begin to make your church a safe place for your average church attendee to begin the path of emotional and spiritual healing, or if you need guidance to improve the freedom group ministries you have already in place, or if you would simply like to tell James your story (he would love to hear it) visit his Web site at www.jamesmreeves.com.